CROWN OF GLORY

And when the prince of pastors shall appear,

you shall receive

a never fading crown of glory

1 ST. PETER, 5:4

Crown of Glory

THE LIFE
OF POPE PIUS XII

BY ALDEN HATCH AND
SEAMUS WALSHE

HEINEMANN

LONDON MELBOURNE TORONTO

William Heinemann Ltd

LONDON MELBOURNE TORONTO

CAPE TOWN AUCKLAND

THE HAGUE

First published 1957
Reprinted 1958

Original American edition published by
Hawthorn Books Inc., New York.
© Copyright 1957
in the United States of America
by Hawthorn Books Inc.

Nihil obstat
        Andreas Moore, L.C.L.
                Censor deputatus
Imprimatur
        Georgius L. Cramen
           Epus. Sebastopolis, V.G.
Westmonasterii, die 22a Augusti 1957

Printed in Great Britain
at The Windmill Press
Kingswood, Surrey

ACKNOWLEDGMENT

ALMOST two years of research were devoted to this book and many thanks are due to the Pro-Secretary of State for Vatican City, Monsignor Tardini; to Monsignor O'Flaherty of the Holy Office; to La Principessa Donatella Colonna, Il Principe Lancelotti, La Marchesa Fumasoni Biondi, Francis Beauchesne Thornton and Fred Kerner for their more than generous help and courteous co-operation. Without the assistance too of the many ordinary people who grew up with His Holiness in his own neighbourhood and with whom were passed many rambling hours, much less might have been achieved. Use has been made of the following literature: *The Papacy* by John Knight; *The Vatican* by Jean Neuvecelle; *The Burning Flame* and *Cross on Cross* by Francis Beauchesne Thornton; *The Pope* by Constantine, Prince of Bavaria; *Eugenio Pacelli, Pope of Peace* by Oscar Halecki and James F. Murray, Jr.; and articles by Bishop Fulton J. Sheen.

Alden Hatch,   Seamus Walshe,

Cedarhurst, N.Y.   Rome, Summer, 1956.

CONTENTS

A*

ILLUSTRATIONS

Between pages 116 and 117

CHAPTER ONE

*

"WE HAVE A POPE"

THE tall, ascetic figure in crimson robes walked slowly across
the sombre room on the third floor of the Vatican. His face
was startlingly white in contrast to his dark hair and the brilliant black eyes that were magnified by his spectacles.
Eugenio, Cardinal Pacelli, Secretary of State and Camerlengo of the Holy Roman Church, moved towards a narrow
bed which was covered with a pall of crimson silk on which
lay the body of Pope Pius XI. At the foot of the bed burned
four great candles; at its head two members of the Noble
Guard stood with drawn swords, the candlelight glinting on
their golden helmets.

Cardinal Pacelli knelt beside the bed and intoned the 'De
Profundis'. Then he rose and lifted the veil that shrouded
the features of the man who lay there. For a long moment
he stood looking down at the still face of Achille Ratti, who
had been his friend as well as his Pope. Then he bent over
and very gently kissed the pure brow. "Achille!" he called.
"Achille!"

Straightening, he turned to the group of cardinals clustered in the doorway, and announced in a low, emotional
voice, "The Pope is dead!"

Thus having confirmed according to tradition the death of Pope Pius XI, Eugenio Pacelli knelt again beside the bed, while the *Maestro della Camera* came forward and drew the Fisherman's Ring from the rigid finger of Achille Ratti, who until that symbolic gesture had been made was, even in death, still Pope.

Then Eugenio Pacelli rose again from his knees and walked slowly from the room.

In the long corridors of the Vatican Cardinal Pacelli's pace unconsciously quickened—there was so much that he must do! In his office he became, temporarily, an efficient executive issuing the orders that started the vastly complicated arrrangements which must be made. First he signed the death certificate, then dispatched messages keyed to the urgency of the moment to sixty-two cardinals in fifteen nations, officially informing them of the death of their Pope and summoning them to Rome to participate in the election of his successor. The messages went by private courier, by telephone and cable, whichever was quicker. The princes of the Church were allowed only eighteen days to reach the Eternal City; for in February, 1939, the world was teetering on the edge of the abyss of war, and the Church, which was the best hope of peace, must not be left for long without a ruler.

Then arrangements must be made for the burial of Pius XI, with all the mournful pomp that tradition and his high place demanded. Innumerable details had to be worked out and the elaborate ceremonies planned and timed so that no unseemly confusion should mar their solemnity.

Meanwhile, Pacelli prepared to receive the princes of the Church, who came to Rome by plane, by ship, by train and automobile. The evening of March 1 was chosen for the conclave, and the lofty arched halls of the Vatican overlooking the Square of St. Damaso were its traditional site.

It must have been with pity in his heart that Eugenio Pacelli watched the preparations, for he knew that the new Pope would face a world-wide turmoil and such difficcult decisions as, perhaps, no man who wore the Fisherman's Ring had ever known before. Thinking of the awful responsibilities which he knew might well be laid on him, he watched the carpenters and workmen carrying heavy timbers and planks across the marble floors, and building wooden partitions in the great galleries of St. Damasus. They divided them into sixty-two enclosures, each of which was in turn partitioned into three rooms, thus forming small apartments. In these the cardinals, each with two attendants called conclavists, would live until a Pope was chosen. In addition, a small hospital was set up. Kitchens were installed as well as accomodations for the Governor of the Conclave, the guards, doctors, apothecaries and servants in attendance.

Since they must be totally secure from disturbance or outside influence, the great windows, set high in the walls, were whitewashed and draped with canvas, turning the interior into a fog-grey twilight. The broad stairs leading from the massive bronze gates of the hall of conclavists were walled off, but in the barrier was set a small wicket, strictly guarded from all unlawful exit or entry by Prince Chigi, the Governor of the Conclave.

Everything was ready for the opening ceremony by March 1. That morning the cardinals assisted at a Mass in Honour of the Holy Ghost in the Pauline Chapel. Eugenio Pacelli fervently implored the Giver of Wisdom to guide him

3

and his brothers in their choice. His thin, aristocratic face was pale and strained as he moved with the others to take up his quarters in the newly built cells. As each came to his appointed place he went inside. Pacelli saw his name over number thirteen, and entered to pray and meditate until the hour of the opening ceremony.

Late in the afternoon, Cardinal Pacelli joined the procession to the Sistine Chapel. In their robes of mourning purple with jewelled pectoral crosses gleaming on white, the cardinals moved slowly towards the chapel, while the ancient hymn, *'Veni Creator Spiritus',* emphasised the awful solemnity of the diminishing hours.

As he moved through the entrance of the Sistine Chapel, Eugenio Pacelli found that emotion heightened its ancient beauty for him. Long narrow windows high up under the roof filtered the fading light of a spring day on to the paintings on walls and ceiling. Behind and above the altar, Michelangelo's dead broke open their graves and shook their shrouds as the seven angels trumpeted the Last Judgment. Above them sat Christ, enthroned as Judge. On the shadowy ceiling and the long walls the story of the Bible from the creation of man to the Life of Christ was portrayed by the immortal artists of the Renaissance.

Sixty-two low thrones were ranged along the walls of the chapel within the sanctuary. The gilt on their arms and high backs gleamed with dull fire, and polished wood shone softly in the fading light. Over each throne was stretched a canopy of purple velvet, heavily fringed; and before each was a small writing desk on which were a candle, matches, paper and pen, and sealing wax. In the centre, between the ranks of thrones, stood a long table topped with green cloth.

4

At the back of the chapel a black iron stove had been placed with its chimney snaking upward through a window. Next day sixty thousand pairs of eyes in St. Peter's Square would watch the protruding end of that chimney for a sign that a Pope had been chosen.

The procession of cardinals, moving over the mosaic floor of the chapel with the faint swish of feet, approached the altar, marvellously inlaid with mother-of-pearl, the altar at which the Pope alone may officiate. Before it Eugenio Pacelli sank to his knees and slowly repeated the sacred oath that he would choose freely and deliberately, uninfluenced by political advantage or any worldly consideration.

One by one the other members of the College of Cardinals repeated the solemn oath. After that the cardinals' assistants, the Governor of the Conclave, the Marshals, and all the attendants and servants swore to observe the rules of the Apostolic Constitution governing the Conclave.

Cardinal Pacelli had one more duty to perform before retiring. He personally inspected the Hall of the Conclavists and the reserved area, making sure that no intruder was present, and that it was sealed off from the world. As he walked through the spacious corridors he could hear bells ringing and the ushers crying *"Extra omnes."* The Conclave had opened, and no unauthorised person might remain.

At half-past seven it was certain that none was there. The great bronze gates were doubly and trebly locked from the outside by Prince Chigi, and from the inside by the cardinal. Then he turned away, and walked slowly back to the seclusion of his cell, and communion with his God.

The next day, March 2, 1939, was Pacelli's sixty-third

birthday. Early that morning all Rome hurried to the Square of St. Peter's. Dignified matrons; messenger boys forgetting their errands; clerical students, whose different coloured cassocks denoted their nationalities; darting school-boys and staid young girls; old people who had come often before; and thousands of black cassocked priests were in the vast throng that flowed down the broad Via della Conciliazione and flooded out over the wide square. From the Parioli district came the rich Romans, formally dressed men, and women furred and bejewelled as though for a reception. Out of the Borgo poured the poor, harassed mothers carrying shawl-wrapped babies, with a ragged brood of children clutching their rusty black skirts; old men, watery-eyed, shuffling eagerly forward; ragged young men and their girls, not less reverent for that.

From the Trastevere quarter, that ancient city where civilisations were piled layer on layer beginning with the little stone village that had guarded the bend of the Tiber against a hostile world up through the ages to the narrow streets of today, darkened by the tall, sombre palazzi of Renaissance Rome, lighted only by an occasional anachronistic neon sign, came the most Roman of Romans, whose ancestors had lived there since Horatius held the wooden bridge at the jutting elbow in the river. Though their character was as heterogeneous as the structure of their city, the wishes of that great crowd were amazingly unanimous. They all hoped that today, after long centuries, they would see a Roman Pope, a man who was, like themselves, a *Romano di Roma*.

Inside the Vatican, though he could not see them, Cardinal Pacelli was acutely aware of the crowd that surged and chattered outside the fortress-like walls. Once more he made his way to the Sistine Chapel, where the voting was about to begin.

When the cardinals were all seated on their shrouded thrones, the senior cardinal drew the names of the three scrutators—the tellers—from a velvet purse. Then, in silence so complete that the faint scratching of pens sounded clearly, the cardinals prepared to register their choice. Each had received a ballot on which was printed in Latin, "I choose as Sovereign Pontiff The Most Reverend Lord Cardinal. . . ."

Though the ballot is secret—each cardinal is required to write the name of his choice in a disguised hand—it has become generally believed that Pacelli wrote the name of Cardinal Vernier on his first ballot. When he had done this, he folded the paper and sealed it carefully with wax.

Then Pacelli walked to the table, where he knelt to pray. Rising, he spoke in a firm voice the traditional words: "The Lord Christ, who shall be my judge, is witness that I choose the one whom I believe should be chosen before God."

Now he placed his ballot on a paten and tilted it so that the folded paper slid into a huge silver chalice set there to receive it. Before and after him the other cardinals cast their votes in order of seniority.

When they had finished, the scrutators took the chalice and shuffled and counted the ballot papers. They announced that the number was correct—sixty-two votes had been cast. Seated at the long baize-covered table, they unfolded the slips of paper and read aloud the name written in the centre of each.

As the names rang out, Eugenio Pacelli heard his most frequently of all. Before the counting was done the

7

scrutators had called "Eugenio Cardinal Pacelli" thirty-five times. He had received more than half the votes on the first ballot, but not the two-thirds necessary to elect.

Out in the square the people swayed and chattered and stared at the blank brick walls of the Vatican, and especially at the small black stovepipe protruding from a window of the Sistine Chapel. Then a faint feather of smoke drifted up, and the whole throng was silent, straining to see whether it would be white, meaning that a new Pope had been elected, or the black smoke of burning ballots mixed with straw showing that no decision had been reached.

The first thin wisp of smoke had no colour in the sunlight. The tension was as tangible as fog. Then the smoke thickened and belched blackly forth, and a vast sigh that was like a rush of wind swept the forest of the crowd.

Within the Sistine Chapel the pens were scratching again; the cardinals moving softly towards the altar to slip the sealed and folded papers into the chalice for another vote. This time it is known that Pacelli voted for Cardinal Dalla Costa of Florence.

Again the scrutators opened the ballots and read them, and this time they called Pacelli's name more than forty times.

So Pacelli was elected on the second ballot, for the count was a bare two-thirds of sixty-two. There was a rustle behind the draped thrones of the cardinals. The Master of Ceremonies moved to proceed with the formal announcement. But those who were there say that Pacelli, greatly agitated, stepped from behind his purple curtains, and humbly begged his colleagues to search their hearts, and vote once again. They accorded him his wish.

By this time it was midday and according to custom there was a recess.

Those who saw Cardinal Pacelli during this interval recall how disturbed he looked, for he knew that he would almost certainly be chosen on the next ballot. Though he had foreseen the possibility of this, the imminent reality filled him with awful dread. Vague thoughts of refusal drifted through his mind, which he tried to banish, recalling that Christ had once said, "You have not chosen me, but I have chosen you."

As he walked through the small, secluded Square of St. Damasus reading his breviary, the members of the Noble Guard noted the strained look of his face, and his hesitant footsteps. Sometimes he looked up from the small book at the tented sky as though he were saying, "Lord, if it be possible let this chalice pass from me!"

When the time came for the voting to begin again, Eugenio Pacelli turned towards the chapel with dragging steps. So shrouded in thought was he that he did not see his way and, stumbling, fell on the marble steps. A rush of guards and fellow-cardinals helped him to his feet. Limping a little and badly shaken, he moved towards the shelter of his throne.

In the tense silence of the chapel, the pens whispered as the voting began again. The slips of paper were piled on the green table, and this time, with a single exception, the scrutators had but one name to say. The vote was unanimous for Pacelli, save for his own ballot, which this time he cast for Granito, Cardinal di Belmonte, Dean of the Sacred College. As the scrutators called his name for the last time, those present say that Pacelli's face was filled with anguish.

When the count of ballots had been verified, the Cardinal-

Deacon rang a bell and opened the chapel door. The Secretary of the Conclave, accompanied by the Master of Ceremonies and the Sacristan of the Vatican, entered. With the Senior Cardinal they approached Pacelli's throne. In firm tones the Cardinal asked, *"Accipisne electionem?"*

For a tremendous moment no answer came. Then in an awed whisper the new Pope answered, *"Accipio!"*

Now each cardinal swept back the baldachins; all the thrones were uncovered except Pacelli's, which still bore the sign of sovereignty.

Again the senior cardinal spoke: "What name do you wish to bear?"

In a firmer voice came the answer, "Pius."

Then the Pope rose to his feet and walked with grave dignity to the sacristy. There he took off his cardinal's robe and was robed in the Papal cassock of pure white, a colour he would never leave off, even in death. He returned to the chapel, and now the cardinals, who had been his equals a few moments before, knelt in turn before him, and kissed his hand and his narrow foot as a sign of their submission to his authority. All the time his lips were moving, and the kneeling cardinals heard him repeating over and over the words, *"Miserere mei!"*—Have pity on me!".

The crowd in the square had swollen until it was packed among the columns of the curving colonnade, piled around the obelisk and swarming back up the side streets as far as vision extended. Suddenly they knew, as by supersensitive human radio. Even before the white smoke poured out of the chimney they knew that a Pope had been named, and by that same mysterious telepathic communication the name

was on ten thousand lips at once—"Pacelli—Pacelli—Pacelli
—Pacelli!" The plume of white smoke confirmed what they
already knew.

The great mass heaved and surged until the obelisk seemed
to sway, and their eyes turned from the stovepipe to the
great balcony under the golden dome of St. Peter's. Soon the
silence was broken by the chant, "Il Papa! Il Papa!" It
kept on and on, rising and falling in a cadence that grew in
intensity until it broke in the middle of a line and stunning
silence fell as two tiny figures in the brilliant uniform of the
Noble Guard stepped through the windows at the back of
the balcony. They moved slowly forward, and over the stone
balustrade threw a white damask cloth embroidered in gold
that shimmered like gossamer in the afternoon light.

In complete silence the guards retired; and a prelate came
forward and reverently carried a processional cross to the left
of the balcony. He was followed by a cardinal in purple
robes who walked slowly towards a hidden microphone.
There was not a whisper of sound in the great crowd. Even
the small children stood, or sat in their parents' arms, as
though bound by the immense pressure of emotion.

The cardinal's clear voice rang across the square, penetrated the colonnades and was carried over the airwaves to
the farthest lands of the earth. "I announce to you a great
joy," he said. "We have a Pope—the Most Reverend Lord
Cardinal Eugenio Pacelli, who has taken the name of
Pius XII."

There was a second of silence that broke in thunder as
sixty thousand persons roared "Pacelli!" The crowd
churned and swirled like the sea in a sub-oceanic earthquake.
Strangers and Romans, carried away by the tide of joy,

turned to each other and embraced, laughing and weeping, because Pacelli was Pope. He was one of them, they knew him well, had heard him preach and seen his gaunt figure walking through their streets—a Roman born of Rome.

Then the babble was stilled as suddenly as an orchestra is quiet at a signal from the conductor's baton. A tall figure in white drifted through a window and came to the edge of the balcony behind the gleaming cloth. Again, as though on signal, came an enormous crash of sound, vibrant with the emotion of full hearts: *"Evviva il Papa! Evviva il Papa!"*

Again and again, like the sound of breakers, the mighty chant crashed against the ancient building of the square.

On the balcony, the Pope raised a narrow white hand, and with one accord the crowd fell silent and sank to their knees. As far as the eye could see, to the banks of the distant Tiber, people knelt in the streets of Rome. With his hand raised in the ancient gesture of benediction, Pope Pius XII gave his first blessing to the city; and to the world.

CHAPTER TWO

A CHILD OF ROME

On a summer day nearly a hundred and forty years ago, Marcantonio Pacelli sat in his study reading a letter. He finished it and raised troubled eyes to look over the rich lands around the town of Onano. The country rolled downhill in the dear familiar pattern of fields of grain, dark green rows of vineyards and the silvery green of olive trees. As he looked he murmured, "Must I leave this lovely earth for the city?"

But the letter was imperative. It was from his uncle, Cardinal Caterini, urgently begging—ordering—him to come to Rome to help with great affairs.

In 1819, Italy was beginning to stir. Ever since the collapse of the Roman Empire thirteen centuries before, it had remained dismembered—a group of petty states and kingdoms, often at each other's throats. Now Italians were becoming conscious of a common birthright, and aspiring to become a nation.

At that time Italy was divided into four major kingdoms. On the north lay Sardinia, ruled by kings of the House of Savoy; and Venezia, centred on imperial Venice clinging to the faded draperies of its ancient splendour. The whole south including Sicily was the Kingdom of Naples under the despotism of a minor branch of the uneducable

Bourbons. The Papal States, the temporal domain of the Pope, which he had held for thirteen centuries, spread across the middle of the Peninsula, embracing Rome and extending to the borders of Venezia.

Marcantonio knew that the rising tide of Italian nationalism threatened the temporal sovereignty of the Church. For centuries his family had battled for Papal supremacy. They had not often reached the dignity of high office, and the throne of St. Peter was beyond their dreams; but many of them had filled the ranks of the Church. They were members of the 'Black Nobility', who owed their fealty to the Pope as their temporal sovereign. Now that his rule was threatened, they had a moral obligation to come to his defence.

Marcantonio's question was purely rhetorical. He knew that he must leave his beloved farm and go to Rome. It was no great distance geographically; but a couple of worlds away in the manner of living.

In Rome, Marcantonio studied church law under the direction of his cardinal-uncle, and it was not long before he was admitted to practice in the courts of the Vatican. He must have been brilliant, for in a comparatively short time he became an adviser to the Pope.

By 1848, Marcantonio Pacelli was one of Pope Pius IX's most trusted officials. In 1851, he became Under-Secretary of Interior Affairs. That was the year of revolution when all Europe burst into flames and ancient monarchies went down like ninepins. In Italy the fire was fed by national pride as well as love of liberty. Garibaldi and Mazzini led the rebels, while King Victor Emmanuel of Piedmont and his sagacious Prime Minister, Count Cavour, guided the tide of revolution away from republicanism towards the idea of a united kingdom of all Italy.

The Pope fled Rome taking Marcantonio with him; then returned for a few years under the protection of French troops supplied by Emperor Napoleon III. In an effort to strengthen the popularity of the Papacy, Pope Pius IX directed Marcantonio Pacelli to found the newspaper *L'Osservatore Romano,* which is still the quasi-official mouthpiece of the Vatican. He remained its editor until his death in 1902, at the fantastic age of 102. (His brother Felice went one better by living in three centuries from 1799 to 1901.)

Neither a newspaper nor anything else could stem the drive of the Italian people towards unity. In 1870, the French troops were withdrawn, and Pope Pius IX retired into the small sacred enclosure formed by the walls of the Vatican. Even there he was pursued by would-be assassins. For sixty years the Pope, thus self-imprisoned, was called 'The Prisoner of the Vatican'.

Long before these tremendous events, Marcantonio Pacelli had married. In 1837, a year when a great plague ravaged Rome, his son Filippo, the second of his ten children, was born.

Filippo followed his father's footsteps in the practice of law. By 1870, he was an imposing man with a heavy drooping moustache, and a rainbow of decorations to wear on his black frock coat. His dark penetrating eyes intelligently surveyed what was for him and all Italians a new world.

For the first time since the Roman Empire, Italy was united. With acute understanding of the meaning and possibilities of this fact, Filippo entered politics. His father had never strayed from Vatican circles, but Filippo, realising the need for liaison between the ancient Church and the new State, moved into the social and political Roman worlds. At the same time he practised church law, and became Dean of Lawyers at the Vatican.

In secular politics he also distinguished himself. He was twice elected a councillor of the municipal government of Rome, and in that position helped to defend the rights of the Church against the overzealous efforts of the new government.

Filippo was also active in the work of his local church, where he taught catechism and tried to educate illiterate parishioners. He distributed books and Church literature and was an energetic member of the Catholic Action.

When Filippo Pacelli married in 1871, he chose a bride who was rather older than was customary, but none the less lovely. Those who knew her at twenty-seven describe Virginia Graziosi as tall, graceful and well poised, with lovely dark eyes that seemed as full of human understanding as her heart was filled with piety.

The Pacellis set up housekeeping in the heart of old Rome, the Via degli Orsini. In the twelfth century, Rome had been a battleground of bandit chieftains, among the strongest of whom were the Princes Orsini. They and the Colonnas and other princely families fought over the ruins of Rome like so many wolf packs. One family seized the Colosseum and built their fortress-palace inside its impregnable walls. Others fortified temples, arenas and other bits of crumbling Roman masonry. The Orsinis built a brick fortress-palace on a rise of ground not far from the old Roman Forum. It is now known as the Palazzo Taverna.

Around this stronghold a cluster of mean medieval buildings grew up, which are still there today. Some are built
on to the walls of the palazzo, and others just straggle off
with no sense of direction. The neighbourhood is a tangle of
alleyways that in the rainy season are as bedraggled as a
slovenly woman. The rain glistens on worn cobblestones and
washes refuse down the gutters, while the inhabitants hurry
furtively along, jumping into doorways to avoid the automobiles and scooters that charge recklessly through the side-
walkless streets.

However, when the glorious Roman sun bursts out, an
almost transcendental change takes places. The old walls
take on the hue and polish of golden amber, the colour of
time itself; and the streets are so full of laughing, chattering
people that the motor vehicles haven't a chance. Old grand-
mothers sit in the doorways talking across just fifteen feet of
cobbles to their neighbours across the street.

The ground floor of every other house is a *baracca* or
small workshop in which the *pater familias* is the proprietor;
and the whole family pitches in; the younger generation as
workers, while the mother is chief saleswoman. They close
up tight at night, when the slatted iron shutters clang down,
and the tortured, twisted maze of streets falls silent; deserted
and dark except for the thin stream of light from an occasional wine shop.

On the fringe of this brick jungle lies the Via degli Orsini.
It is a short street, but wide by comparison with the alleys,
and leads to the small Square of the Clock. On the far side
of the Square is the Chiesa Nuova, the New Church, so
called because it is only about four hundred years old.

On the left side of the street, as you leave the Square, is

No. 34, known as the 'Palazzo Pediconi'. It was never a palace, but it seems palatial in contrast to its neighbours. The Filippo Pacellis rented the third-floor apartment. The rooms were spacious, with high, ornate ceilings. Tall windows in the back looked out on a pleasant courtyard full of small trees and flowering shrubs. In the far corner a fountain was set into the wall; and in relief on the stone-work was the face of a cherub, chubby and smiling. Above his head stood a protective eagle. The continuous stream of clear water from the fountain made a deliciously cold noise as it fell into a stone trough. On summer days passers-by liked to peer at it through the high, arched entrance of the palazzo. This entrance was closed at night by enormously tall, thick wooden doors.

On March 2, 1876, Eugenio Pacelli was born in this typical Roman dwelling, the third child of his parents. Two days later, he was baptized in the small, oval Church of Saints Celso and Julian just around the corner from the Pacelli's apartment. The family and close friends gathered at the Palazzo Pediconi and walked in a gay procession to the church, Filippo Pacelli in his black broadcloth. Prince Albert, glittering with medals, led the way, carrying the tiny infant. Beside him walked his pretty wife. Close behind them toddled their children Giuseppina and Francesco, the latter in a Fauntleroyan costume of black velvet and white lace collar. Behind streamed the others laughing happily.

Only the infant was not in a festive mood. It is reliably reported that he howled vigorously as his priestly great-uncle, Monsignor Giuseppe Pacelli, named him Eugenio Maria Giuseppe Giovanni.

There is a story in the Pacelli family that one of the

Pacellis' best friends missed the ceremony. Monsignor Jacobacci had a morning when everything went wrong. By the time he could get away it was too late for the baptism, so he hurried directly to the Palazzo Pediconi to offer congratulations and join the feast that would follow. The Pacellis had not returned, and he stood waiting in the early afternoon sunshine until he saw them turning the corner, a laughing, joyous crowd all dressed up in their best clothes, the men in black broadcloth, and the women and girls in their colourful finery. He hurried towards them, and apologised profusely for being late.

"We missed you," Filippo said gaily, "but anyway you have now arrived."

"May I see the child?" asked Monsignor Jacobacci.

Pacelli put the baby in his practised arms. Very gently he pulled aside the froth of lace that covered its tiny face, and looked long and earnestly at the blue-lidded eyes and the tiny wisp of black hair that escaped from under a tiny cap. As he felt the warmth of the new body an indescribable tenderness filled him.

People who tell this story say that a sudden hush fell over the little group as the old monsignor stood holding the child. He looked at the baby's father with unseeing, yet far-seeing, eyes and said in a strange, clear voice, "Sixty-three years from today the people in St. Peter's and all Rome will loudly praise this child."

*

CHAPTER THREE

A MIND IS FORMED

FROM the moment a child notices anything at all his character begins to be formed. In this his mother plays an almost solo rôle as she leads her baby out of the dark, booming confusion that surrounds it.

Virginia Pacelli was not only a devoted mother, but deeply religious. She truly believed that the only reason we are born into this world is to serve God. So little Eugenio Pacelli was conscious of God almost as soon as he was conscious of hunger; and certainly in that household prayer was more important than food. As soon as he could speak, his mother taught him to say his baby prayers at her knee. And his father's example was equally devout.

By the time Eugenio was five years old and ready to start school, the Pacellis had moved to Number 19, Via della Vetrina, the Street of the Window. This was deep in the crowded area that surrounded the Palazzo Taverna.

The pious Pacellis would not dream of allowing their son to attend a kindergarten or any other school supported by the State. Anti-clericalism and new ideas on philosophy, they feared, had penetrated even to that level. So they found a school they were sure was run in the old familiar way. It was conducted by the Sisters of Divine Providence, and situated conveniently close to the Via della Vetrina. In this gentle atmosphere the sisters extended the peace and contentment of spirit that Eugenio found at home.

Little Pacelli was already showing a marked leaning towards a religious life. In Rome it is the usual thing to see small shrines in houses, on the street corners, even in offices, dedicated to the Madonna or some favourite saint. The Pacelli home was no exception, but Eugenio wanted his own special shrine. He made it himself, with an altar on which he put a fine white damask napkin, pieces of lace, and silver vases that he joyfully wheedled out of his mother and adoring older sister. He kept the vases filled with flowers, and when he played at religious ceremonies, candles burned in silver candlesticks on his altar.

Aparently Genio's one secular passion, then and all his life, was music. He learned to play the violin at a very early age, while his younger sister, Elizabetta, was equally precocious on the piano. Apparently the only arguments the devoted brother and sister ever had concerned the interpretation of a favourite composition. On such points Eugenio had strong views.

Eugenio liked to hear tales of the Gospel and the early martyrs. His family tell the story of how one day his uncle told him about a missionary priest who, after long suffering, was finally crucified by his tormentors. The little boy looked so solemn at the end that his uncle began to be afraid he had pitched it too strong. "Don't you like the story, Genio?" he asked.

Eugenio looked away from his uncle, and said in a small, doubtful voice, "I think that I, too, would like to be a martyr."

"Well . . ." his uncle began.

But Genio brightened, and said decisively, "Yes, I would like to be a martyr, but—without nails!"

When Eugenio was ten, he had learned all the Sisters of Divine Providence could teach him. Just about this time Giuseppe Marchi, who had a fine reputation as a teacher, started a private school in his house in the Piazza di Santa Lucia de Ginnasi on the far side of the Chiesa Nuova. His ability brought him quite a few boys of the 'Black Nobility'. The school seemed made to order for Eugenio.

Indeed, the moment he came under the intelligent guidance of Professor Marchi, Pacelli's mind opened its doors. Marchi grounded him well in the classics, and he delighted in the works of the ancient Greeks, and in the history of his own great city. But his special ability was in languages. He picked them up seemingly without effort, and could soon converse fluently in French and German, and had some English. To these he added many others in the course of his life.

It was inevitable that Pacelli's physical growth should not keep pace with his intellectual development. His brain seemed to burn his body out. This was not because he did not try to be athletic. He was too intelligent not to realise that he needed a strong body to serve God. He learned to swim and went boating, and he took long walks. His favourite sport was riding through the byways and level fields of the golden Campagna, for while he rode it was easy to think. These things he did from a sense of duty, as other boys study.

On his way home from school Eugenio had to pass the Church of the Gesu. It stood opposite the house where, in

1540, Saint Ignatius Loyola, founder of the Society of Jesus, lived. In those days it was called 'Madonna della Strada'— 'Our Lady of the Way'. Because of the Saint's connection with it, the small church became the great building it now is; but the original shrine with its beautiful, ancient painting of the Madonna was kept intact.

One day Eugenio was so late coming home from school, that Signora Pacelli became really worried. She went out and looked anxiously up and down the narrow, twisting street. There was no sign of him; so she hurried towards the school. She did not know what turned her feet into the Church of the Gesu, but instinctively she went in. She paused to bless herself with Holy Water from the font. Then, looking in the direction of the painting, she saw Eugenio's dark head outlined by the still candle flames. She went and knelt beside him, and in a little while they left the church together.

"It was unkind to worry me," she said, and he told her he was sorry.

"What did you do in the church for such a long time?" she pursued.

"I don't know," he answered. "I just tell Her everything."

Eugenio first assisted at the Sacrifice of the Mass in his own church, the Chiesa Nuova, where he became an altar boy for his cousin, Don Vincenzo Cirilli. He had a perfect record of attendance, for he considered it a great honour and joy to be allowed to wear the cassock and surplice and to assist the priest.

Sometimes Father Lais officiated. He was a man born out of his time, who, before they were given a name, realised the value of youth clubs. He gathered together a group of tough teen-agers and would-be teen-agers, and by natural leadership and human understanding trained them in citizenship and right living. They used to meet in a large room in the church building, where he let them play if they liked, or listen to his informal talks. He often took them out in the country for long walks and rough and tumble games. Eguenio belonged to this group and loved it.

Father Lais was also a well-known astronomer. He had rigged up a telescope on the roof of his apartment. The boys used to gather there on fine autumn evenings when the stars were especially brilliant in the deep Roman sky to study the vastness of the universe. Those waiting their turns at the telescope played the game of counting the 'tears of St. Lawrence' as shooting stars are called in Italy.

Eugenio would have liked to stand for hours gazing through the eyepiece at wonders that seemed to bring him even closer to God.

When Eugenio was fifteen, his father decided that it was time for him to think of choosing a profession. Eugenio had no definite ideas on the subject, but Filippo Pacelli had very definite ones. He wanted his son to be a lawyer like himself.

So Eugenio was entered in the Liceo Quirini Visconti. In 1891, this liceo, or high school, had a fine reputation for scholarship; but it was a very different sort from the pious education to which young Pacelli was accustomed. It was state-controlled and staffed by professors whose ideas on politics and religion were extremely 'modern'—which then meant nineteenth-century materialism. Most of them were anti-clerical and 'open-minded'—open especially to the insidious doctrines of Karl Marx. Italy, and particularly

Rome, its political and intellectual centre, was fertile soil for materialistic isms. The government of the Church having been cast aside, the city was drunk with its new freedom, like an adolescent boy who rejects the advice of experience and must try everything for himself.

It was in fact virgin soil for free thinking—the kind of soil especially adapted to the growth of communism. So Marxian theories filtered down from the universities to the high schools. The atheistic materialism of the new German thought was the fashion; and many of the professors and teachers were avowed communists. They had a misguided missionary zeal to inculcate these ideas on their pupils.

It must have been like the shock of an icy plunge to young Pacelli after being sheltered in a sort of intellectual incubator. However, Eugenio neither fell for this specious thinking, nor did he reject it blindly. Rather he examined these new ideas and found them wanting. In his thinking he was helped by Pope Leo XIII's encyclical, *Rerum Novarum*, 'Of New Things', which was published the year he entered the lyceum.

The encyclical sharply drew the difference between the theories of Marx, which were based on class struggle, and the principle of Christianity, which led to democracy. Eugenio read it and understood. He could see how the basic concept of communism must lead to self-destruction. It seemed to him that the social turbulence boiling in Italy was due to this speciously appealing, but basically false, doctrine. On the other hand, he thought that democracy, based on Christian belief, would lead to that social peace which eventually would evolve into international peace. He was convinced that social peace was completely impossible under Marxist doctrine and practice.

25

He decided that communism was negative, as evil itself is negative. He even had a dim prevision of the horror and bloodshed it could produce. He resolved to face it, to fight it, and never to condone it.

The antagonistic atmosphere of the lyceum was a good thing for Eugenio. It honed the edge of his mind to brilliance, and rid him of soft thinking. It also offered him the advantages of genuine scholarship that opened the way to the higher levels of learning, and taught him how to pursue them. He was much too sensible to disregard materialistic philosophy just because he thought it wrong. Instead he studied it carefully in order to combat it. But unlike many of his fellow students, who thought themselves more tolerant, he also read the *Rerum Novarum* and the Confessions of St. Augustine.

In this connection there is an anecdote of how Pacelli's history professor, a communist, gave the class an assignment entitled, "Whom do you consider the greatest hero in history?"

It was perfectly plain that if you wanted to please the professor you would submit the name of a revolutionist. Pacelli wrote the name of St. Augustine as his choice.

This was meat for the professor. He read the name aloud and added, "Will the gentleman who made this puerile choice stand up."

Pacelli arose. He was so tall and thin, that he looked as though a gust of wind would blow him over, but his eyes blazed through his steel-rimmed spectacles.

"What is this?" demanded the professor. "Some sort of joke?"

"I am ready to prove to you that my choice is no attempt

at wit," Pacelli said, "but is based on the truth. And I'm prepared to back it up with logic."

Then he turned to the class and asked, "Has anybody here read St. Augustine?"

An embarrassed silence was his answer. Looking straight at the professor, who was also uneasy, Pacelli went on, "If you had, you must surely know that he was one of the deepest thinkers of Christian antiquity."

The professor gladly let it go at that.

Though Eugenio frequently disagreed with his professors, they gave him honour marks. Again, languages were his speciality. His fellow pupils remember him as quiet and reserved. Despite this handicap—for such it is in any school —he was well liked, and respected for his willingness to come out of his shell and fight for his principles whenever they were challenged—which was quite often.

However, it was all very exhausting. At the end of his second year at the lyceum, Pacelli was more gaunt than ever. He caught cold easily, and had a continous cough. For once he was glad when school ended. Though his spirit was as ardent as ever, every nerve and muscle and organ of his body cried for rest.

The Pacelli family still owned the little farm at Onano, and Eugenio's mother proposed that he go there to build himself up for another strenuous winter. Eugenio was delighted. On 'the lovely earth', which his grandfather had left to come to Rome, he would renew himself. And there he would make the decision that he had refused to face until now.

*

CHAPTER FOUR

EUGENIO DECIDES

LIFE was wonderfully slow in Onano. Its tempo had not changed in two thousand years, and the mechanics of living hardly differed from the days when Cincinnatus beat his sword into a ploughshare which must have been very similar to those that Eugenio saw the curved-horned oxen drag through the black earth. Each morning at sunrise the peasant farmers and all their families trekked down from the hilltop town to the fields and vineyards. In the golden sunshine of late afternoon they came back, weary but still gay; some riding on their tiny donkeys or in the slow ox-carts, others walking barefoot up the hill.

Eugenio walked a great deal, roaming the olive groves of the foothills and the dusty white roads that meandered between fields and vineyards. Sometimes he rode one of the farm horses, and nearly every day he had a plunge in a cold mountain stream. And all the time he was thinking hard.

Although he was studying to be a lawyer, he had not definitely decided on a career. Now that he was eighteen, he knew he could put it off no longer. He was aware of his father's wishes in the matter; but he also knew that Filippo Pacelli would not put any pressure on him, for the jurist believed that freedom of choice is God's gift to man. Eugenio had not discussed the subject with his mother; for he knew in his heart what she wanted.

Young Pacelli was very much attracted by the legal profession. He had the type of mind suited to it: a searching, painstaking mind, careful in its assessment of truth. To be a prominent lawyer was a worthy aim. He would be following the tradition of his family, his famous grandfather and respected father. He was too sensible to have false modesty; he was conscious of his ability to succeed in that career.

On the other hand, Eugenio felt a strong compulsion towards the Church. Spiritual and moral rewards were much more important to him than money or fame. And he knew that all the new ideas and intellectual ferment had reduced the number of young men who were willing to dedicate their lives to God. The need for priests was very great. They were required to act as guides for the boys and girls who were growing up; they were needed by everyone as spiritual advisers. Particularly were they needed, he thought, to mediate between the embattled classes; to strike a balance between haves and have-nots; to conciliate, reason, and, above all, to comfort.

Pacelli did not actually reach a decision at Onano. When he came back to Rome, his family was delighted at how tanned and rested he looked. They did not press him as to his future plans.

The young man felt the necessity for contemplation before finally deciding. He applied to the Canons Regular in the Via Nomentana for permission to enter their house for a short time. He wanted to make a retreat; to retire from the world and live in complete silence for four days.

The room he occupied was as bare as a room could be—a

cell in fact. Here he passed the greater part of his self-imposed imprisonment. The days were spent in religious exercises. He rose very early and attended Mass in the chapel. Except for evening devotion, the rest of the time was passed in solitary prayer and meditation. After those four days he had no doubts as to what was right. He decided to become a priest.

The day after his retreat Pacelli walked home through the early morning streets, unconscious of the hubbub and bustle, because of the calm certainty within himself. His mother greeted him at the door, and knew by his tranquil face what he had decided.

If Filippo Pacelli was disappointed he did not show it, for he was assured that his son had made the decision after full consideration. In fact, it was no great surprise to any of the Pacelli family or their friends. They had all thought it more than likely that Eugenio would become a priest—he had all the signs of his vocation.

Now that Pacelli's career was chosen, there were all sorts of technical details to be arranged. First a seminary must be selected, and permission to enter it obtained. Eugenio's parish priest gave him a strong recommendation as a young man likely to persevere in his vocation and to be a worthy addition to the ranks of the Church.

The next thing was to be accepted by the bishop of the diocese. A young man cannot just decide to become a priest, enter a college and be ordained. He has to be 'adopted' by his bishop; that is, the bishop takes him as a candidate for work in that diocese. There is no such thing as a 'free-lance' priest.

With his fine record and recommendations, the bishop

was, of course, happy to accept Pacelli. The young man duly entered the Capranica as a clerical student.

The Capranica College was founded by Cardinal Capranica in 1457. Even today it still retains a distinctly medieval aspect. A grim exterior, punctuated by dots of windows, faced on the little Piazza Capranica, which was only a stone's throw from the Pacellis' home in the heart of Rome of the Middle Ages.

It was a small college—no more than fifty students could live within its walls. But its quality was the highest. Many famous men had studied there who later achieved their reputation in various aspects of the Church; some through learning, and some as cardinals; while a few attained to the Triple Tiara of Papal sovereignty. However, young Pacelli had no great aspirations. Those who knew him say that he pictured himself as a parish priest serving the people.

Eugenio entered the Capranica early in November, 1894. As he passed through its high and heavy portals, and climbed the wide marble stairs leading to the first floor, he saw a large crucifix a little above him on the wall. The cross was wood, and nailed to it was a wooden figure of Christ when His agony was over. The figure was slender and well-proportioned, in the pride of manhood. In spite of the blood flowing from the thorns that pierced the smooth brow and trickling through the thin line of moustache and beard, the grasping tension of stiffened fingers and the spreading crimson of the open wound in the side, it gave a feeling of repose that comes after a hard-won victory.

Eugenio was exalted by this figure, and always when he entered or left the college, as on that first day, he looked up at it and murmured a short prayer.

After he had registered, he was shown to a room on the second floor. It was the fourth on the left of the corridor and was very tiny. The furniture consisted of a little narrow bed that would certainly tempt no one to linger in it; a table, a chair, and a cabinet for his clothes. In the corner was an iron tripod supporting a wash-bowl and water-jug.

The room had one small window that looked out on an ancient courtyard, thick with lemon and orange trees, but ragged and uncared for.

The three floors used as living quarters for the students were divided into almost exactly similar rooms. The second floor housed the youngest class, who moved up as they grew older. The seniors lived on the third floor. In that room, or one like it, Pacelli expected to spend the next four years. At eighteen he was older than most of his fellow students, but Eugenio was determined to work very hard to make up for lost time.

The regimen at the college was very strict. Just outside of Pacelli's door was a big bronze bell, like a ship's bell. At six o'clock every morning its clangour blasted him out of bed and echoed through the corridors. At six-thirty there were communal prayers and meditation in the chapel, which was on the same floor as his room. It was very small and awkwardly arranged. The backless wooden benches ran at right angles to the altar, which was set out from the wall and lighted from the back by a large window, whose tinted panes of glass let in only weak light even in summer.

At seven o'clock the students went to Mass; and at seven-thirty they had breakfast. As is usual in Europe, this was merely a hot cup of milk mildly flavoured with coffee or chocolate.

For the next four and a half hours there were lectures to attend. These were held at other colleges in Rome, as there were no classes in the Capranica. At twelve-thirty the students got their first real meal of the day. The food was good enough, but it was both monotonous and rather meagre.

After dinner was the time of relaxation, for in Italy the siesta prevails even in the cloister. Pacelli and his fellows could rest or study in their rooms if they liked, or they could leave the college precincts and walk through the town, but only in groups. Probably so that their minds would not be distracted from their mission, they were not allowed to visit their homes without special permission. Though this was seldom refused, the students were not expected to ask unless there was a real need.

After this recess there was another three to four hours of lectures before supper. Then came a further period of recreation, which consisted of meeting in the common room and talking shop, that is, about their studies or theology.

Nine-thirty was bedtime, but the students were allowed to study by the light of oil lamps in their rooms. Before and after each meal, and again before retiring, they all met in the tiny chapel for prayers and devotions.

The rules of the community were based on mutual trust and respect for the vocation of the priesthood to which each student felt himself called. Eugenio Pacelli appreciated this communal life and the time it gave him for the things he liked to do best—to study and to pray.

Eugenio Pacelli had always been thin and predisposed to catch cold. The rigorous life at the Capranica made him even more gaunt. Then, too, he drove himself as none of the other students did, for he had three years to make up—the three years he considered wasted since they had been devoted to preparation for a legal career and not for the service of his Master. Much later Pacelli realised that those years had not been wasted at all, but had been useful, perhaps divinely ordained, to enable him to serve more perfectly the necessities of the Church.

After about a year at the Capranica, the strain proved too great for Pacelli's frail body. He caught a dreadful cold, which evolved into a deep cough that racked him day and night, shattering even the quiet of his hours of prayer and meditation. When at last he consulted his family doctor, Eugenio received a verdict that was even more disheartening then than it is now—he was threatened with tuberculosis. Nothing would save him but rest and fresh air. Even then one could not tell.

Feeling completely crushed he went back to the farm at Onano.

The time of his convalescence was one of the most trying of Eugenio's whole life. Sometimes in his discouragement he felt that his illness was a sign that he had been rejected by God. At others his mystical nature inclined him to feel that this was but one more test of the strength of his character, of his fitness to serve. Then his courage would return and he would relax almost fiercely, consciously willing health to flow back into him. The hardest thing of all was to limit himself in the extent of his daily devotions in order to conserve his strength.

After a few weeks Eugenio decided to go to Rome to see his doctor. He borrowed the local postman's horse and cart to make the trip to the station. When they reached the inn at the foot of the hill, the horse stopped dead, for here the postman always shared a bottle of wine with his equine companion. Pacelli ever impatient of delay, rushed into the inn, and bought a whole litre of wine, all of which he fed to the balky animal. Grateful for his double ration, the horse went off at a gallop. This soon slowed to a trot, and then an amble, zigzagging across the road. Eugenio did his best to steer a straight course, but it was no use. Finally the horse stopped still, spread his legs wide apart and fell sound asleep. Eugenio walked home meditating on the evil of excessive zeal.

As it had before, the pure air and serenity of Onano worked its natural miracle. Eugenio's body filled out and became firm again; his skin tanned, and he no longer felt the horrid, skin-pricking rise of fever in the afternoons. His cough quieted to an occasional short bark. When he felt his vitality rising higher than it had for many years he went back to Rome.

This time the doctor was much more encouraging. The disease was arrested, perhaps even conquered, though the victory was still not complete. Under no circumstance would he consent to his patient going back to the ascetic life of the Capranica. It was the bitterest of blows to Pacelli. How then could he ever hope to become a priest?

While he pondered unhappily at home, word of his situation was carried by friends to the Holy Father. Pope Leo XIII already knew something of his story, and was aware of the young seminarian's deep piety and brilliant scholastic record. He determined that such a youth should not be lost to the Church because of a technicality. For the only time in the whole long history of the Capranica, the Pope granted a student the extraordinary dispensation to resume his studies for the priesthood as a day student, without being subject to the rigid discipline of community life.

So Eugenio returned to a modified regimen of study. Being the sort of youth he was, he was not puffed up by such special privilege, but rather humbled by it and fiercely determined to be worthy.

It was at about this time, in 1896, that Eugenio Pacelli, who is perhaps the most travelled Pope, made the first of his many trips abroad. He went to Paris with Father Lais, who had remained a close friend, to attend a conference of astronomers in Paris. On the train he watched the grand but ragged landscape of Italy give way to the ordered abundance of French fields and forests, and with the changing aspect of the country human nature seemed to change, from the happy-go-lucky Italian peasants to the dour farmer-proprietors of France. Such a difference in a few hundred miles brought home to Pacelli how infinitely varied humanity must be in the vastness of the world, and how splendidly universal was the Church which could embrace and unify the human spirit in its many manifestations.

In Paris, Pacelli met and listened to astronomers from all over the world. For the first time he caught a glimpse of the scientific mind in action, and his respect for the vision and intellectual courage of these men who were probing the mysteries of the universe made him forever their disciple. Nor did the pragmatism of the scientific method shake his faith. Rather it confirmed and enriched his faith to know that man had been created with such a wonderful capacity

for acquiring knowledge and evaluating it without precon-
ceived prejudice.

On the way home, Father Lais and Eugenio travelled
through Belgium, Holland and part of Germany. And again,
as he crossed the borders of those extremely individualistic
nations, Pacelli marvelled at the infinite variety of human
nature. The journey was the beginning of the rich experience of peoples everywhere which he brought, at last, to the
Chair of Peter.

After he left the Capranica, Pacelli went on to the famous
Pontifical University of the Roman Seminary. Stronger now
than ever before, with the flame of his spirit adequately supported by his rejuvenated body, he made so brilliant a record
at the university, that on the day of his graduation, Pope Leo
sent for him to come to his apartment in the Vatican.

Through the splendid corridors, past the elaborately
accoutred guards, Pacelli walked, all trembling with excitement and awe, his vellum diploma clutched in his hand. At
the end of all that magnificence was the Pope's simple apartment, and a little old man in white extending his hand.
Almost overcome with emotion, Eugenio knelt to kiss the
Fisherman's Ring and receive the congratulations of Pope
Leo XIII.

Eugenio Pacelli was ordained a priest on Easter Sunday,
April 2, 1899, in the Church of St. Mary Major. It is impossible to describe, or even imagine, the waves of exaltation and humility that swept his soul during the long ritual
by which he was accepted and consecrated to the service of

God. When it was over, though he would not himself have thought it, he was as pure and dedicated as St. Augustine himself.

On the following day, in the Borghese Chapel of the same church, Father Eugenio first offered the sacrifice of the Mass.

＊

CHAPTER FIVE

"THEY ALSO SERVE

HIM..."

AFTER his ordination, Father Pacelli went back to Onano. Though he was impatient to begin his ministry, the mental and physical ordeal he had been through had taken a lot out of him. He had to rest or collapse again.

The hot summer days passed quietly in the country, as the figs and olives slowly ripened under the blue sky. Don Eugenio, as he was now called, read a great deal. Despite the calm around him, he was restless with an inner drive to be about God's business, which even his love for Onano could not assuage. He had chosen to become a priest through that compulsion, and he knew that he would only attain fulfilment in the pursuit of his calling.

As soon as he felt strong enough to return to Rome, he threw himself into the life of the parish. His post was that of curate at the Chiesa Nuova, where he had first served Mass and first realised the greatness of the priestly vocation. He went about his duties with quiet zeal. Though he had already taken his doctorate of theology, no work was beneath his dignity, no teaching so simple that he would not give his best. In fact, his greatest joy was to gather the children of the parish around him and, talking on their level, explain the meaning of the catechism, teach them simple prayers and listen sympathetically to the confused woes of childhood. He also spent long hours in the little confessionals listening to the sins and sorrows of that over-crowded neighbourhood. Frequently at night he would be aroused by a sick call and stumble sleepily through the dark alleys to bring comfort to the sufferer; often to someone who had known him as a boy, and who lay sick, perhaps dying and very frightened.

On Sundays, Don Eugenio sometimes preached at the Chiesa Nuova. Some who remember those days picture him mounting the pulpit with rapid, nervous steps, but speaking with the firm assurance of a Roman to the Romans he knew so well; expounding doctrine to his people, admonishing or exhorting them with an inspired certainty that clothed his youth with authority.

Eugenio loved his work, and when he thought of his future he imagined himself in charge of some similar parish, working thus and striving for his people with contentment.

But though his ambition was so simple, his mind was too fine an instrument to be neglected—no good Christian may hide his talent. In the little spare time he had, Eugenio went to the College of Apollinaris where he won his doctorate of Canon and Civil laws, *summa cum laude*. He had previously taken his doctor's degree in philosophy. Thus he ended the preferred simplicity of his life.

Now the Church as an organisation was as keenly aware of its need of fine instruments to serve its high purpose as any corporation. From Pope Leo XIII down, its chief dignitaries had their eyes on young Pacelli. Particularly his friend and patron Vincenzo Cardinal Vannutelli brought him to the attention of the Vatican, without Pacelli's knowledge. The young priest had shown himself to be unusually intelligent, and, unlike many intellectuals, he was painstaking and conscientious in his work. He had a thorough knowledge of three important languages, French, English and German; and was a doctor of theology, philosophy and canon law. Finally, they took into account that he came from an aristocratic country family who had faithfully served the Church for generations. The latter consideration was not snobbery, but simply the realistic estimate that such a background made the young priest even more valuable. It was no great surprise to anyone—not even to Pacelli—when Monsignor Gasparri paid him a visit.

The monsignor was Secretary of the Congregation of Extraordinary Ecclesiastical Affairs, which is the Vatican Foreign Office.* There is also a Home Office called the Congregation of Ordinary Ecclesiastical Affairs, which, in 1901, was headed by Monsignor Giacomo della Chiesa. The overall head of both departments was Mariano Cardinal Rampolla, Secretary of State.

At this time Pope Leo XIII had partially succeeded in restoring the international prestige of the Holy See. Throughout the long history of Christendom the Holy See had always been a tranquillising influence in the troubled affairs of nations, called in to act as mediator between countries on the verge of conflict, or to promote peace among those already at war. But ever since the beginning

* For the convenience of the reader, this book substitutes the term "Foreign Office" for "Congregation of Extraordinary Ecclesiastical Affairs" throughout.

of the so-called Age of Reason in the eighteenth century, and particularly during the early nineteenth century, its prestige had been waning.

This was due to many causes, among them the materialistic philosophy of the era. The 'Age of Reason' produced the great revolutions and wars that, aiming for liberty, upset established governments and in many cases left chaos in their wake. The rage of the revolutionists was frequently directed at the Papacy. Pope Pius VI was taken prisoner by the French Republicans, and Pius VII suffered the same fate under Napoleon.

Then came the irresistible urge to unify the Italian people in a great national State, which resulted in the formation of the Kingdom of Italy and the absorption of the Papal States. Stripped of his temporal power and the beautiful Quirinal Palace, Pope Pius IX retired to the Vatican, physically defeated but spiritually undaunted. For many years thereafter the new government of Italy remained suspicious that the Church was trying to regain temporal power over the lost Papal States.

Leo XIII was a new kind of Pope. Trained in the school of practical diplomacy, he had won the respect of the diplomatic corps as Nuncio in Brussels, and had made himself popular in that capital, which was somewhat anti-clerical. He came to the papal throne with a clear-eyed picture of what was happening in Europe, the surge forward of democratic principles as the old monarchies crumbled.

Though he also formally demanded the return of the Papal States and was unbending in his attitude towards the Italian Government, he did not repine over the fall of kings. Rather, he saw an opportunity for leadership by emphasising the Christian teaching that all men are equal in the sight of God, and that the labourer is worthy of his hire. One of his first moves was to open the archives and libraries of the Holy See to students and teachers from all over the world.

Leo XIII's great ambition was to restore the prestige of the Vatican as a force for peace. Working on a purely spiritual plane, he sought to restore the Holy See to its great traditional rôle of unbiased mediator in disputes between nations.

The first thing to do was to reverse the trend that had the Vatican sinking into a sort of diplomatic isolationism. The new Pope went to work to reinvigorate diplomatic relations between the Holy See and other nations. The first sign that this new policy was paying came in 1885 when Spain and Germany appealed to the Pope to mediate a dispute over the possession of the Caroline Islands in the Pacific. It was a relatively minor matter in international affairs, but an important indication that his hopes were justified.

In 1899, Czar Nicholas II of Russia, put forward a plan for a general peace conference of European nations, and asked the Pope's support. Leo gave it with all his heart. It was decided to hold the conference at the Hague, and Protestant Queen Wilhelmina of Holland wrote to the Pope asking for his further support. This he was anxious to grant, but the nervous new Government of Italy refused to allow the head of the Catholic Church to be represented at the conference.

However, the willingness of nations to meet and discuss peace was one of the hopeful signs of the times, which were indeed more civilised than any before or since. In view of all this, Pope Leo decided he needed a corps of trained diplomats to represent the Holy See. He instructed Cardinal

Rampolla to recruit likely candidates and to school them. One of the first names the Pope proposed to Cardinal Rampolla was that of Eugenio Pacelli.

After receiving his instructions from Cardinal Rampolla, Monsignor Gasparri paid his portentous visit to Pacelli. Though he was not surprised, the young priest was very doubtful when Gasparri offered him a position in the Vatican Foreign Office. "This is not what I became a priest to do," he said. "When I made my decision I had no thought of the Church needing the sort of work you describe. My desire was and is to work among the people of my parish, this one or another. I have no other ambition."

The monsignor smiled into the earnest black eyes behind the young man's spectacles. "They also serve Him, who work in the administration of His Church," he said. " 'In my Father's house there are many mansions.' We feel that you will be more valuable because of your special qualifications in our department than at your present work. Also, you will have a little spare time for the parish. We do not want our officials to lose touch with the people. But we want you. Will you accept?"

"What else can I do, Father?" said Eugenio. "Yes, I will come and serve to the best of my ability, but I am disappointed. It is not by my wish."

From that moment Don Pacelli's life changed radically. No longer did his neighbours see the young priest walking every morning towards the Piazza Navona and his college. Instead he headed briskly in the opposite direction towards the Tiber and the Castle of St. Angelo. He crossed the river by the Ponte Umberto, and entered the Borghi, a dilapidated part of Rome which at that time surrounded the Vatican— it was later partly torn down by Mussolini's slum-clearance project. The word Borgo is a corruption of the English word borough. In the early Middle Ages, this district was where the Anglo-Saxons settled, hence its name. It is thought to have been founded by King Ine of Wessex, who built the church of San Spirito there early in the eighth century. In 1901 it was one of the poorest quarters of Rome, where open sewers still ran through the middle of the narrow, cobbled streets which were choked with rubbish and crawling with children, who nevertheless seemed to flourish like flowers in the mire. They overflowed the doorways of the ancient tenements, and played in packs in the filthy alleys. As Pacelli followed these tortuous man-made gullies, he thought of the work he could do in this seething volcano of humanity.

Instead, he hastened on to the Gate of Bronze at the end of the right-hand colonnade of St. Peter's Square which led to the offices of the State Department.

Before 1870 this department had been quartered in the Quirinal Palace, later the residence of the Kings of Italy and now of the Italian Presidents. When Rome was lost to the revolutionaries, the secretariat fled to the Vatican where it was housed in the third storey of the rambling palace.

Pacelli entered through the massive doors, passing the guard-house where the Swiss Guards now keep modern rifles with fixed bayonets stacked, though they still carry medieval halberds on sentry duty. He rapidly mounted the broad marble sweep of the Scala Regia, and crossed the courtyard of St. Damaso. After climbing another flight of stairs, he reached the modest office of the secretariat. Here he was allotted a small table at which he seated himself apprehensively.

Pacelli's first position was that of a minor clerk, an *apprendista* it was called, which might be loosely translated as apprentice. His work was mainly to write unimportant letters—the Vatican was not yet equipped with typewriters—and to copy reports from nuncios all over the world. It could not have been better training; for Pacelli's retentive mind stored up a vast knowledge of the complex problems faced by the representatives of a truly global Church. Soon he could smile at his naïveté of a few months before. Here indeed was work to be done that was vital, not only to the Church, but to all mankind. Yet Father Pacelli still wished that he could live and work in a simple parish—he has wished it all his life.

Though Eugenio Pacelli was only an apprentice clerk, it is evident that the Pope's eye was on him. Soon after he entered the Secretariat of State in 1901, Pope Leo appointed Pacelli as his envoy to carry his personal condolences to King Edward VII of England on the death of Queen Victoria.

It is surely a very unusual apprentice who learns his trade in such exalted circumstances. At the Court of St. James's, Pacelli, who was 25, was most likely the youngest of all the diplomats who hurried to carry the sympathy of the nations of the world to the court of courts on the death of a sovereign who had become a symbol of the stability and grandeur of the British Empire, and had given her name to an era in history. Certainly he was the most plainly dressed. In that assemblage, which, despite the tokens of formal mourning, blazed in gold-embroidered diplomatic and military uniforms, their breasts glittering with the stars and crosses of their distinctions, the tall young man in the plain black cassock of a simple priest must have been as unique as a penguin in a flock of flamingos. Pacelli was quite aware of his oddity, and completely unconcerned, since the livery of God was to him more glorious than any secular splendour. He moved at ease among the famous figures of the Victorian Age, modest but dignified. Word came back to the Vatican of the fine impression he had made with his quick smile and friendly warmth.

*

CHAPTER SIX

"I BLESS PEACE, NOT WAR!"

Pope Leo XIII died in 1903. He was sincerely mourned by everyone, for his inspired leadership had done much to rejuvenate the Church. Father Pacelli was especially sorrowful, for Pope Leo had been his protector and friend, the first truly great man he had known.

The official world of the Vatican, especially those in the foreign office, hoped that Cardinal-Secretary of State Rampolla would be elected to the papal throne, for they believed he would carry on the dynamic policies of Leo.

However, this was not to be. On the first ballot of the cardinals assembled in the Sistine Chapel, Rampolla received twenty-four votes, by far the largest number. Much to his own surprise Giuseppe Cardinal Sarto, the beloved peasant priest whom Leo XIII had made Patriarch of Venice, received five votes. On the second ballot the number of votes for Cardinal Sarto doubled and Rampolla gained but one. Sarto had thought that the first vote was in the nature of a pleasant compliment. But when it was doubled he became very unhappy, for he considered himself too simple a man, and altogether unworthy, to be the Supreme Pontiff.

At the next session, which was held early the following morning, a dramatic incident took place. Before the voting began, Cardinal Puzyna, Archbishop of Cracow, stood up to address his fellow-princes of the church. In a grave voice he said, "I am honoured to present a memorandum from His Majesty the Emperor Franz-Joseph of Austria, King of Hungary." He then read a document in Latin from the Emperor stating his objections to the election of Rampolla, and insisting that Austria had the right to veto the election of any candidate for the Papacy.

This much disputed 'right' was called 'exclusion'. It had been claimed by the Emperors of Austria and other Catholic countries for centuries, and, though never admitted by the Holy See, it had not been defied. In the present case the Emperor's message had been inspired by the Italian Government, who feared Rampolla because of his great political ability.

The moment Cardinal Puzyna stopped reading, Cardinal Oreglia was on his feet. Holding up his hand to quiet the angry buzzing of his colleagues, he said firmly, "This message has no place here, either officially or unofficially. We will not take the least notice of it."

Then Cardinal Rampolla spoke, saying, "I greatly deplore the grave wound a secular power has inflicted on the dignity and freedom of the Sacred College. For my own part nothing more honourable or pleasing could happen to me."

On the next scrutiny of the ballots it was found that Cardinal Rampolla had twenty-eight votes—a gain of three; but Cardinal Sarto's count had again more than doubled to a total of twenty-one.

After the vote was announced, Sarto, his face ashen, rose.

In a trembling voice he implored the cardinals, "Please, I beg of you, don't vote for me. I am unworthy, incapable of filling this great office. Please forget me!"

As the conclave recessed, the cardinal hurried to the Pauline Chapel to pray. He realised that the cardinals would probably elect him, and the thought was agony to this humble man who had believed himself unworthy even to be a bishop, and who had protested strongly when Pope Leo had raised him to the rank of cardinal. The awful responsibility of the Papacy seemed more than he could bear. It was utterly unbelievable to him that the Sacred College should think him worthy, for he felt sure that he was not. In his spiritual agony he wept and implored the Saviour and His blessed Mother to alter the cardinals' resolve.

For long hours he remained there on his knees. At last he felt a light touch on his shoulder, and turning saw young and handsome Archbishop Raphael Merry del Val, who was pro-secretary of the conclave, kneeling beside him. In the dim silence of the chapel Merry del Val said softly, "The Lord Cardinals have sent me to beg that you will not refuse election if it is offered to you."

In a broken voice the cardinal said, "I cannot do it. I know that I am not able or worthy."

The young archbishop rose from his knees, and putting his hand on the bent shoulder of the cardinal said with deep emotion, "Courage, your Eminence, take courage. You, who were able to guide so well the gondola of Venice, will surely be able to steer the bark of St. Peter in Rome."

The white-haired cardinal raised his blue eyes to look into the chiselled Spanish face of the young archbishop. A tide of sympathy flowed between those very dissimilar men. The cardinal rose from his knees and clasped Merry del Val's arm. It was the beginning of a famous friendship.

But all the archbishop's arguments could not sway Cardinal Sarto. That evening many of the cardinals came to him, among them Cardinal Gibbons of Baltimore, who promised the help and growing strength of the Church in America. Last of all came Cardinal Satolli. To him Sarto pleaded, "I am old. The burden will kill me."

Satolli replied sternly, "Even so! Remember the words of Caiaphas, 'It is expedient that one man should die for the people.'

"You are obliged to consider the will of the Sacred College," Satolli went on. "It is unthinkable that you should refuse."

Tears spurted from Cardinal Sarto's eyes. "I must accept God's will," he said.

The following morning he was elected Pope, taking the name of Pius X.

Giuseppe Melchiorre Sarto came from the little village of Riese in the Province of Treviso of northern Italy. He was born poor, and he lived poor. His parents were peasants, barely wresting their subsistence from three hilly acres of land. His father eked things out by acting as messenger at the town hall, for which he received fifty soldi a day. Beppe, as the boy was called, began to help support his family at an early age. He attended the one-room school-house in the village, and then worked for hours in the fields. When he got home he had to help with the household chores. It was a long day for a little boy.

However, the parish priest recognised that Beppe was

worth helping, and coached him to win a scholarship at the high school in Castelfranco, four miles from Riese. Every day Beppe walked the eight miles to school and back with a piece of bread in his pocket for lunch. Even when he got a pair of shoes, he walked barefoot in the country, saving them to put on when he entered the town.

At Castelfranco, Beppe won another scholarship to the seminary of Padua. He arrived to begin his studies wearing a worn-out soutane given him by the kindly parish priest.

Giuseppe Sarto was ordained in September, 1858, and was appointed curate in the hamlet of Tombolo, where he served for nine years, sharing his house and what meagre food he could buy with the poor of the parish. Then he was made parish priest at Salzano. From then on his fame as a preacher and his works of charity brought him swift advancement. He became a canon at the cathedral of Treviso, and then Bishop of Mantua. Finally, the Pope made him Patriarch of Venice and a cardinal.

Beppe's hair had turned silky white by now. He had a square, ruddy face in which bright blue eyes sparkled with joyous affection for his people. His speech was salted with shrewd earthly wit. Indeed, Beppe had not changed inwardly at all. His luxurious palace in Venice was open to everyone. They tell the tale of a peasant who wandered in, and poured out his troubles to a courteous stranger with whom he talked for an hour before he discovered his comforter was the cardinal.

Cardinal Sarto continued to give away everything he had, his income, the gifts he received, and his clothes. He maintained ten students at the seminary, and often visited all the poorer quarters of the city, helping and giving.

However, he was also a good administrator and a progressive thinker. He helped to arouse the social conscience of Venice, and to found working men's societies, and he reinvigorated the fast-dying lace industry of Burano. Many years later Pope Pius XII called him, "An ardent flame of charity and a bright light of sanctity."

It is often said that Pius X owed his election to Franz-Joseph's use of the 'Right of Exclusion'. Rather, the Emperor's interference almost turned the scales in favour of Cardinal Rampolla. It was the cardinals' realisation of the earthly goodness and spiritual strength of this man, who later became the first Pope to be canonised in two hundred and forty years, that inclined them to vote for Sarto.

Nevertheless, Pius's first act as Pope was to denounce the Right of Exclusion, and it was never heard of again. His second was to make Merry del Val a cardinal and appoint him Secretary of State.

The young Spaniard was ideally chosen to complement the unworldly character of the 'peasant Pope'. Though Pius X was a cultured man with considerable knowledge of music, who had proved himself an able administrator in Venice, his saintliness and simplicity made him believe, perhaps too strongly, in the innate goodness of people. He was not prepared to cope with unscrupulous men. On the other hand, his new Secretary of State, though truly devout, had a realistic knowledge of the world, and especially of the labyrinthine diplomacy of his era.

Merry del Val's father had been Spanish Ambassador to the Vatican and his brother represented Spain at the Court of St. James's. His mother was an Englishwoman. He had been born in England and mostly educated there, attending

Ushaw College, set among the coal mines of Durham. He came to Rome to finish his studies, and was ordained for work in the Diocese of Westminster.

Merry del Val wanted to go back to England and his diocese, but the Vatican kept him in Rome, where he became one of the youngest and most astute of the diplomats of the Holy See. He was extremely useful for missions to Canada and England. When in Rome, he was often seen at the North American College, where he played a very good game of tennis, and made firm friendships among staff and students. Later he presented the college with one of its treasured possessions, a magnificent billiard table.

At thirty-seven, Merry del Val was the youngest man to have been appointed Cardinal Secretary of State.

In the first year after the election of Pius X, Don Pacelli served out his apprenticeship. In 1904, he was promoted to the rank of *minutante,* which is a sort of confidential secretary. In that position he attended high-level conferences, prepared secret reports, and drafted important state papers. In short, he was taken completely into the confidence of his superiors.

In the same year Pacelli was appointed a Papal chamberlain and made a monsignor. This title is not conferred by any special religious ceremony; but is granted by the Pope as a mark of distinction. The award is made known by a 'letter patent', which advises the recipient that he is entitled "to all the privileges of place and rank that may accrue".

There are precious few privileges except that, if the new monsignor is in the personal service of the Holy Father, he may work even harder than before.

However, Monsignor Pacelli now doffed the plain cassock of a simple priest. His cassock was still black, but it was made of finer material with all the edges and cuffs piped with red and a long line of red buttons extending from chin to feet. A small shoulder cape was attached to the cassock, and the stock beneath its collar was changed from black to red. When in Rome he wore silver buckled shoes.

In 1905, Pacelli was further honoured by being made a Domestic Prelate, a title of honour and distinction conferred by the Pope for services rendered to the Vatican.

Gasparri, now a cardinal, was still head of the Vatican Foreign Office and these two worked ever more closely together. All his colleagues and the Pope himself leaned heavily on Pacelli's judgment.

But all of Monsignor Pacelli's time was not occupied by high-level diplomacy. He continued his work at the Chiesa Nuova, where he still taught catechism, heard confessions, and occasionally preached. He also continued studying, and became a part-time lecturer in canon law at his old alma mater, the Apollinare.

In addition he conducted frequent seminars at a private school for girls in the convent of the Sisters of the Assumption and acted as spiritual adviser at a home for working girls called the House of St. Rocca.

Such a schedule clearly indicates that Pacelli had finally conquered his physical weakness. Put it down to sheer will-power, for certainly he had not pampered his body, but rather driven it beyond the limits of normal endurance.

The decade from 1904 to 1914 was tranquil on the surface, though, underneath, the pressures of national ambition and the armament race between England and France and the

German Empire were building up to the explosion of World War I. During these last years of serenity, Eugenio Pacelli played a great part in a tremendous task which Cardinal Gasparri had undertaken at the direction of Pius X. It was no less than the codification of the Canon Law, a labour beside which the projects of Hercules seem simple. For church law had been built up during a thousand years of edicts, papal bulls, instructions, decrees, regulations and precedents, each probably applicable to its era, but often contradictory and by now in such a state of confusion that many ecclesiastical authorities considered codification absolutely impossible.

To bring an ordered system out of such a legal tangle required not only a sound knowledge of jurisprudence, but an imaginative affirmation of the doctrines of the Church.

Cardinal Gasparri had chosen the right man for his assistant. Monsignor Pacelli organised the work, and soon an army of priests all over the world were busily searching through their archives. Their findings were sent to Rome where they were sifted, indexed, and ultimately codified by Gasparri and Pacelli. The work was finally finished and the first draft sent out to the bishops just after the death of Pius X in 1914. It gave Monsignor Pacelli a legal knowledge equal to that of any man who has ascended the papal throne.

Even those labours did not keep Pacelli tied to a desk. Twice again he went to England, the first time as assistant and adviser to Cardinal Merry del Val at the International Eucharistic Congress of 1908. Pacelli's third visit to England was in 1911, as a member of the Papal delegation to the coronation of George V.

In that same year the Catholic University of America in

Washington, having heard of his vast labours in the jungle of church law, offered him the Chair of Roman Law. He wanted very much to go, for he had a far-sighted understanding of the growing power and importance of America, and realised, as many Americans of those days did not, that the United States would soon be a great factor in international affairs.

Pope Pius, himself, and Cardinal Merry del Val told him they could not spare him. Disappointedly he refused the offer. Soon afterward, in 1912, Monsignor Pacelli was made acting Secretary of the Vatican Foreign Office.

The summer of 1914 was very hot, and apparently serene. But the tensions of the armament race were becoming acute. Advised by Merry del Val and Pacelli, Pope Pius X was anxiously awake to danger. Again and again he warned Europe of the peril of 'sudden fearful wars', that might spring from the diplomatic chess game the great powers were playing, with battleships and armies as the capital pieces, and the lives of their subjects as the pawns. Typically, no one heeded the words of the saintly old man in the Vatican.

The pistol shot that killed Archduke Francis-Ferdinand at Sarajevo was the flash that fired the European powder barrel. Helplessly the Pope, helplessly Merry del Val and Pacelli watched the drift towards war, slow at first, and then, as the days of July ran out, with terribly quickening pace. Now, the very men who had played with the fire, the statesmen of Austria, Russia, Germany and France tried to halt the spreading flames. But the momentum of mobilising armies and unbridled speech was too great. Kings and

Emperors, the royal cousins of Europe, sent pathetically affectionate, desperate telegrams to each other begging for peace; but family ties were too frail to stem the onrush. On July 28, 1914, the declarations of war went out, and on the frontiers of Europe little flickering flashes of rifle fire from border guards grew as the reserves poured out, and the crash of cannon punctuated the rattle of machine-guns in the spreading holocaust.

On a hot, desperate day, the Ambassador of the Austro-Hungarian Empire asked an audience of the Pope. The Holy Father received him sitting on his throne in the Hall of Audience. Beside the throne stood Cardinal-Secretary of State Merry del Val and the tall thin figure of Monsignor Pacelli.

The Austrian Ambassador in full court dress advanced and kneeling kissed the Fisherman's Ring. Then he made known his mission. "Holy Father," he said, "thousands of Catholics will march in the armies of Austria and Germany. Through me, His Majesty the Emperor of Austria asks that Your Holiness bless his armies in this struggle."

The frail old man in his pure white robes seemed suddenly filled by the fires of youth. His knuckles whitened on the arms of his chair, his blue eyes blazed and his voice resounded through the room as he said, "I bless peace, not war!"

Then he rose and tottered towards his private apartment on Pacelli's arm.

Three weeks later, on August 20, 1914, Pope Pius X died.

*

CHAPTER SEVEN

MISSION TO GERMANY

As men by the tens of thousands died in an ever-widening arc of fire from the Marne on the west to the Pripet Marshes on the east, Giacomo Cardinal della Chiesa, Archbishop of Bologna, was very quickly elected Pope, and named himself Benedict XV.

The new Pope was a small, dynamic man, with a clear precise mind. So short was he that even the smallest of the three white papal robes prepared in advance by the Vatican tailor completely engulfed him. Around the papal court his affectionate nickname was 'Il Piccoletto'—'the little one'. In temperament and experience he was quite different from his predecessor. He had had twenty years of training under Cardinals Rampolla and Merry del Val in the Vatican Foreign Office, and was, in fact, a career diplomat. Now he had need of all his skill.

Benedict's first move showed his appreciation of the necessity for the most expert assistance. He appointed Cardinal Gasparri Secretary of State, and Monsignor Pacelli moved up to Secretary of the Congregation of Extraordinary Ecclesiastical Affairs. Thus Benedict acquired a proven team to advise him on the delicate relations of the Holy See with the passion-blinded statesmen of the warring powers. Certainly the name of the department that Pacelli headed was now justified—never in history up to that time had the Vatican been involved in such extraordinary ecclesiastical affairs.

Whatever cynicism there may have been among the emperors, kings, prime ministers and generals of the belligerents, there was no question that their subjects and citizens—German or French, British, Russian or Austrian—passionately believed in the justice of their respective causes. The Pope was acutely conscious of this fact; and, though he might have his private opinion as to who the aggressors were, as Vicar of Christ and head of His Catholic Church, he could express no sympathy towards one side or censure of the other, lest by condemning the leaders he become associated in the minds of their millions of followers with partisanship, and thus shake their allegiance to the Church and their very faith in God.

People being the way they are, his impartial attitude excited the suspicions of both sides. In fact, the one thing that the Central Powers and the Allies agreed upon was that they wanted no 'meddling' by the Holy See. So strong was this feeling that when Italy came into the war on the side of the Allies in May, 1915, she had stipulated in the secret Treaty of London that France, England and Russia should agree to back Italy in "preventing the representatives of the Holy See from taking any steps whatsoever in regard to the arrangements for peace or the settlement of problems connected with the war."

Even neutral America, led by such genuine idealists as President Woodrow Wilson and Secretary of State William

J. Bryan, took a peculiarly jaundiced view of any papal proposal for peace.

Benedict was much too astute a diplomat not to realise that his hands were bound by the prejudices of the leaders of the fighting nations. He knew that there was virtually nothing he could do to stop the holocaust, though that did not keep him from trying. But if he could not arrest the course of the war, there were many things he could do to alleviate its consequences. He placed most of the business of relief in the hands of Monsignor Pacelli.

Pacelli was especially fitted for the job. He knew personally many of the diplomats on both sides with whom he must deal in order to get permission for acts of mercy; knew how to instruct his representatives as to the best way of approaching them. He also knew the needs of the people themselves, not just the over-all pattern of hunger and sickness and destruction, which were universal, but the special local requirements of all those sharply individualistic nations.

The worst situation was that of the prisoners of war. Conscription had produced armies of millions of men, far larger than ever before in history. In the rapid German advance through Belgium and France, the prisoner bag was tremendous. The German General Staff had not foreseen this. They simply did not know what to do with hundreds of thousands of captives; so they just herded them into barbed-wire stockades where they began to die like fish stranded on a beach.

On the Eastern Front the situation was even worse. The Russians had taken many thousands of German prisoners in their advance into East Prussia; and the notoriously inefficient Czarist Army was hopelessly baffled by the problem. In addition, they were, if anything, less humane than the Germans. So the plight of their prisoners was incredibly miserable.

Pacelli determined to use the entire hierarchy of the Church to cope with these conditions. Orders went out from the Vatican to the bishops of all dioceses in which there were prisoner-of-war camps to see to it that the priests who spoke the language of the captives were enabled to contact each of them personally, and to establish communication between them and their families. Furthermore, the bishops were instructed that no distinctions were to be made between race, nationality or religion. All were to be taken care of as well as was humanly possible.

As soon as the priests got to work, reports began to come back to Pacelli of the many wounded among the prisoners who were dying from lack of care and the despondency of their condition. He promptly opened negotiations with all the belligerents for the exchange of wounded prisoners and interned civilians. Since these unfortunates were a source of embarrassment and a drain on their captors, and no military good to their own countries, the various governments were willing to listen to reason. As a result of Pacelli's efforts nearly 65,000 people were returned to their homes.

In all this Pacelli worked closely with the International Red Cross and the Swiss Government. Neutral Switzerland opened her sanatoriums to wounded and tubercular soldiers of all nationalities.

Nor did Pacelli's army of working priests content themselves with helping those in the camps. Throughout the belligerent countries and those that were occupied they ceaselessly searched for news of the missing and the dead; and the information they obtained was sent to the Vatican and the Red Cross to be forwarded to the families of the victims.

In addition, vast quantities of medical supplies were sent to field and base hospitals. Large amounts of food were supplied to the peoples whose homes had been overrun by the tide of war.

For three years Monsignor Pacelli directed this great network of relief activities. He thought of it as a job to be done once in a lifetime. Had he realised that he was only learning how to handle even heavier responsibilities in a yet more terrible war, the load might have been more than he could bear.

By January, 1917, after nearly three years of mass slaughter with no decisive results, everybody but the generals was sick of war, and there were signs that even the military were looking for a way out. Pope Benedict XV felt that now there might be a chance for direct action for peace to succeed.

In December, 1916, President Wilson had queried the belligerents as to the terms on which they would consider making peace. With Gasparri and Pacelli the Pope carefully studied their replies and came to the conclusion that there was sufficient common ground to offer a faint hope of peace. Working closely with Pacelli for several months, he drew up his own peace plan.

At this time the question arose as to how best to present it to the nations at war. The Pope did not want to launch it at all if there were no chance of its having at least a hearing. He needed to sound out the various governments ahead of time. This would have been simple enough if he had had diplomatic representatives in all their capitals; but he did not. The nearest thing to an official contact with Kaiser Wilhelm II's Government was the Papal Nuncio to King Ludwig III of Bavaria. In February, 1917, the Nuncio, Archbishop Giuseppe Aversa, died. The Pope decided to replace him with a man who he hoped would be able to get to the Kaiser himself and lay the groundwork for peace. Pacelli was the obvious choice. His appointment was announced in April, 1917. Pope Benedict decided to consecrate the new Nuncio Archbishop of Sardes.

On May 13, 1917, a little group of spectators were gathered in the Sistine Chapel. The solid Sunday black of their clothes contrasted oddly with the brilliant colours of the magnificent murals that adorned its walls and ceilings, and the ceremonial robes of the bishops and monsignori. The sombre little group consisted of the Pacelli family. Only Eugenio's father, Filippo, who had died six months before, was missing. They had come to see Eugenio consecrated as Titular Archbishop of Sardes.

In the strong cool daylight from the long windows set high in the walls the candles on the beautiful altar reserved for the Pope burned with a faint reddish flame. The doors were flung back, and the small ecclesiastical procession entered. Eugenio walked behind his new mitre, which was carried on a white silk cushion. Behind him came Monsignor Achille Ratti, and crimson-robed Cardinal Gasparri. Last of all was the small, vibrant figure of the Holy Father.

Ordinarily, Cardinal Gasparri would have consecrated his subordinate, but Pope Benedict XV decided to perform the ceremony himself as a special mark of his love for Pacelli, and an acknowledgment of the difficult and onerous mission which he had undertaken.

The procession divided as it reached the sanctuary of the Sistine Chapel and allowed the Holy Father and Monsignor Pacelli to approach the altar, on which the seven candles burned. The vestments of His Holiness, the chasuble, gold mitre, jewelled pectoral cross and gloves of sheerest silk lay in an ordered heap of gold-encrusted white on the altar-stone.

The Pope and the monsignor bowed to the cross and to each other; then knelt on the crimson cushions and prayed silently. While the Pope was being vested, Pacelli moved to a small altar that had been set up at one side for his use.

When Pope Benedict was ready, he seated himself on a small faldstool with his back to the altar. Monsignor Pacelli was escorted by the two assistant bishops to three stools that had been arranged in a semi-circle facing the Holy Father. The bishop on Pacelli's right then requested His Holiness in humble tones to raise Monsignor Pacelli to the Episcopate. He presented the document to the Pope who passed it to his secretary to read aloud.

When this was done, Pacelli, kneeling with bowed head at the feet of his Pontiff, took the oath of allegiance to the Holy See. Then he again seated himself on his stool and according to ancient custom was closely examined. He publicly affirmed his belief in the doctrines of the Church and declared his readiness to assume the onerous responsibilities of the Episcopate and his willingness to defend those doctrines and discharge those responsibilities even in the face of death itself. Then, pale with emotion, he kissed the Fisherman's Ring.

The Mass began. At the side altar, Pacelli took his part until, just before the Gospel was read, he turned and prepared to receive the rite of consecration. Approaching the main altar where the Holy Father knelt, Pacelli prostrated himself, and lay full length at the feet of the Pope, as the latter recited the long Litany of the Saints, in which he invoked the Apostles and all the early martyrs and saints by name to help and to give inspiration to the new bishop.

At the end Pacelli rose, then knelt again, and the great book of the Missal was opened and placed against his head and shoulders. The Holy Father and the assistant bishops then let their extended hands rest lightly on the dark head which was bowed before them, and together they implored the Holy Spirit to enter into him.

Pacelli's head was now bound with white linen cloth while the choir chanted '*Veni Creator Spiritus*'. Benedict made the sign of the Cross on the head of the newly-consecrated postulant. He applied the oil from the Holy Chrismal, and then Benedict blessed him with the threefold blessing.

Blessed and anointed, with a linen shawl draped around his neck, Eugenio Pacelli stood almost overcome with emotion. To one of his mystic nature, he seemed indeed transported and at one with the great company of the elect; yet altogether unworthy. Hesitantly, he put out one hand from the folds of linen and received the crozier—the shepherd's crook, symbol that in correcting vice he might be severe, that he must judge without anger, and yet encourage and soothe the souls of his flock. Still holding the crozier, he extended the third finger of the same hand on which the Holy Father slipped the episcopal ring in token of his authority.

66

The concelebration of the Mass continued, Pacelli and his Pontiff partaking of the same Communion and drinking from the same chalice. Towards the end, the mitre was placed on the new bishop's head symbolising that, like a knight of old, he took upon himself the championship of the cause of Christ, that with this helmet of salvation he might appear terrible to the enemies of truth.

Now completely vested, he seated himself on the faldstool of the Pope and, with His Holiness at his right hand, joined humbly in the singing of *'Te Deum Laudamus'*, in which the voices of all the company joined and swelled in triumphant tones of thanks to their Creator.

As the ceremony ended, Archbishop Pacelli, wearing his mitre, the staff in his hand, turned towards his mother. Virginia Pacelli in her widow's weeds knelt to receive her son's first episcopal blessing.

Archbishop Pacelli wasted no time in starting on his mission. Each day lost meant that some thousands of men were killed or wounded in the deadly stagnation of trench warfare—the average weekly casualties of the British Army alone were more than twenty thousand at this time. He left Rome for Bavaria on May 20, 1917, taking with him Pope Benedict's peace plan which he and Cardinal Gasparri had worked out so carefully with the Holy Father.

The plan was necessarily vague as to detail, but specific on principles. It embodied proposals for progressive disarmament; a pact among all nations for the abolition of conscription; the substitution of arbitration for an appeal to war; 'sanctions' against any nation that refused to accept the judgment of the arbiters; and the freedom of the seas.

More specifically, the plan proposed the restoration of all

occupied territories; and provided for discussion of the status of disputed areas, such as Alsace and Lorraine, in which 'due weight' should be given to the wishes of the population.

It also proposed that the independence of Belgium be guaranteed; and that Poland should be granted "that full and perfect liberty which is called independence."

Actually the Pope's plan foreshadowed President Wilson's Fourteen Points, which sixteen months and a million casualties later were accepted by all the belligerents as the basis of peace, and became the cornerstone of the League of Nations.

The Archbishop of Sardes arrived in Munich on May 25, and went directly to the Nuncio's official residence, a neo-classical palace on the Briennerstrasse directly opposite the Brown House, which later became the infamous cradle of Nazism. During World War II both buildings were destroyed by the same huge bomb.

The very next day, Pacelli, who was not the man to waste a moment in the pursuit of peace, secured an audience with King Ludwig III of Bavaria. And, two days later, in a royal carriage, accompanied by the Royal Chamberlain with a clanking outrider trotting ahead, the Archbishop was driven to the famous old Royal Palace, which had been redecorated in the extreme rococo style by the King's ancestral name-sake, mad King Ludwig. Its frivolous gaiety contrasted oddly with the tired anxious faces of the Bavarian Court.

Pacelli was received in state. Members of the royal household awaited the Nuncio in the great hall. Passing up the Black Staircase, which was lined by troops of the Royal Bodyguard in field-grey uniforms and spiked helmets, he came to the vast ornate throne room, where the King and his Foreign Minister, Count von Hertling, awaited him.

Pacelli lost no time in making the object of his mission clear. In his opening address he told the tottery, white-bearded king of the Pope's desire to act as intermediary in peace negotiations, and added, "The task of collaboration in this work of peace has been entrusted to my weak hands in a period that has no parallel in history."

After his formal reply, King Ludwig, who had little patience with ceremonial, took the Nuncio to his study for an intimate talk. Pacelli, aware that Ludwig was his best chance of reaching the German Emperor, spoke eloquently and logically of his mission. He urged that, with Ludwig's support, it might be possible to achieve the peace so much desired by the Holy Father; a peace founded on the Christian principles of love and justice.

King Ludwig was heartily tired of war, and frightened by his own prospects. He agreed to use what influence he had with his imperial master to arrange that Pacelli be received by the German Government.

As a result, the Nuncio was invited to Berlin to confer with the Imperial Chancellor, Theobald von Bethmann-Hollweg on June 26, 1917. From the Anhalter Station Pacelli drove through the sombre streets of Berlin directly to the German Foreign Office. The Chancellor took him at once to his office and himself closed the door.

After a few compliments, Pacelli firmly stated the conditions under which Pope Benedict hoped that peace might be made. The Chancellor was worried, almost distraught, for he realised how desperate Germany's situation was and knew his imperial master's uncompromising nature. He is said to have moaned aloud when Pacelli spoke of the possible restoration of Alsace-Lorraine to France. But he was greatly impressed by the earnest, logical words of the Nuncio.

The fact is that von Bethmann-Hollweg was too reasonable a man to suit the megalomaniacal mood of Kaiser Wilhelm's final period. Indeed, the Chancellor was on his way out. But he had just enough influence left to arrange an audience for Pacelli with the Emperor.

It took place on June 29. Doubtless in the hope of flattering Pacelli, the Kaiser sent a private car to convey the Nuncio and his Uditore, or aide, Monsignor Schioppa, to his military headquarters which were in the castle of the ancient Rhineland town of Kreuznach. Guided by an aide in a beautifully cut field-grey uniform and a spiked *pickelhaub* helmet, Pacelli and the Uditore passed through medieval stone corridors guarded by rigid sentries who clashed their bayoneted rifles in salute. They were shown through an ornately furnished grand salon to a room which held a few chairs and a plain desk with a field telephone on it. War maps lined the high walls.

The German Emperor stood behind his desk, with his withered left arm resting on the hilt of his cavalry sabre, and the Grand Cross of Iron Cross dangling from the collar of his field-grey tunic. He greeted the Archbishop with the minimum of respect due to his office and forthwith began to talk in rapid, explosive French, interlarded with German words.

Indeed, throughout the interview, the Kaiser's manner was a curious blend of arrogance and exculpation. He dwelt at length on how his efforts for peace had been thwarted by the stubbornness and foolishness of his enemies. But despite the Kaiser's rather whiney description of himself as a much-wronged peace-lover, Pacelli could see no sign of softening in his attitude. Here was a man still absolutely sure of himself and the power of his armies, still arrogantly confident of victory.

When the Nuncio finally got in a few words about the Pope's peace plan, the Emperor with a slight sneer suggested that he might have more success if he presented it to a Catholic Power.

The discussion was interrupted by an elaborate luncheon, at which Prince Henry of Prussia and von Bethmann-Hollweg were also present. Pacelli, seeing that his discussion of peace terms would get nowhere, switched the conversation to a plea that the Kaiser put an end to the practice of shipping Belgians into Germany as semi-slave labourers. At this, the Kaiser suddenly became reasonable—apparently he was not completely indifferent to world opinion. At his most charming, he promised Pacelli to put an immediate stop to the practice. And on this faintly more conciliatory note they parted.

Despite his discouraging reception at the Imperial Court, Pacelli's hopes rose again when he went to Berlin to see the new Chancellor, George Michaelis, who on July 14 replaced von Bethmann-Hollweg. Michaelis declared that the German Government was ready to talk peace on the basis of the Pope's proposals. Although the Allies' reaction to the papal feelers had been rather coy, Benedict decided to publish his plan on August 14, 1917. The German papers promptly denounced it as being dictated by England, while the French journals declared that it was made in Germany.

Indeed, when the Nuncio received the long-winded evasive note in which Michaelis replied to the Pope's proposals, German Deputy Erzberger, who was with him, reports that Pacelli with tears in his eyes said, "Your poor country. All is lost!"

Days of anxiety, exhaustion and frustration followed for the Archbishop. Interview piled on wearisome interview. Diplomatic promises were offered and quickly withdrawn. Pacelli passed through the gamut of emotions from high hopes to blank despair. In the end there was only despair.

The fact is that neither side wanted to negotiate because they were both completely confident of victory: the Allies because the United States with its vast, untapped reserves of fresh manpower and industrial production had entered the war; and the Kaiser because the Russian Army had been completely demoralised by the Russian Revolution, and, with the German divisions thus released, he was sure he could knock France and England out before the American Army took the field.

By October, Pacelli came to the bitter conclusion that Michaelis had been simply playing cat-and-mouse with him. With no hope left of immediate action, Pacelli returned to Rome to report his failure to the Holy Father.

*

CHAPTER EIGHT

"THE MONSTROUS FACE
OF COMMUNISM"

AFTER a very short stay in Rome, Archbishop Pacelli went back to his post in Munich. Even though there was nothing to be done for peace, there was a tremendous job to do in alleviating misery. He virtually spent the next year on the road, travelling around Germany, which was sinking further each week into the grey misery of war and the stupor of imminent defeat.

There was hardly a prisoner-of-war camp or hospital that he did not visit, bringing not only material gifts of food and medicine from the Holy See; but, since he could talk with all but the Russians in their own language, bringing also a message of comfort and hope.

During the final months of war the Allied blockade had reduced the German people to a point just above mass starvation, and many unfortunates fell below that level. Though Pacelli had small use for the militarists, the plight of the civil population moved him deeply. He has said that the sight of starving, homeless children roaming the streets and countryside sent an actual physical pain through his heart.

To help them and the unhappy German poor, who, normally living at a subsistence level, were ground down by the pressures of defeat to actual starvation, he organised a great relief campaign.

Through all that terrible winter and the final despairful summer, he went from place to place speaking to people of all religions, giving them hope of Divine protection, and somehow raising the means for material aid. He was undeterred by storm or bitter cold, or the immense difficulties of travel in a country fighting a desperate final battle against overwhelming odds, with a collapsing internal economy. That his frail physique withstood the strain is proof that the spirit truly can reinforce failing flesh.

The work of mercy that Pacelli performed is still remembered in Germany today.

The end came for Germany in November, 1918. The Kaiser and his bemedalled court fled to Holland in a special train, while the humble citizens, who now headed the hastily organised republic, undertook the thankless task of surrendering Germany to the victorious Allies.

Though the guns fell silent on the Western Front, there was no peace in Germany. Millions of German soldiers, slogging back home through the autumn rains with their rifles and ammunition still in their possession, felt that they had not been defeated in the field, but betrayed at home. As the cold deepened, the misery of the population became even worse than in wartime owing to the chaotic condition of the economy and the fact that the Allies refused to relax the blockade which denied food to the starving people. Bitterness swelled into revolution incited by the Bolshevists, who, having gained control of Russia, were quick to exploit misery in their plan to communise all Europe. Red flags flew over the mobs that stormed and took the city halls in the great port cities of Hamburg and Kiel.

The Communist Revolution came to Munich on February 21, 1919, when Kurt Eisner, head of the temporary Democratic-Socialist Government, was assassinated. After six weeks of sporadic street fighting, on April 4, 1919, the Communist mob seized the Bavarian Government and declared it a separate Communist State. At this point all the diplomats in Munich packed their belongings into automobiles and trucks and scampered across the frontier to the comparative safety of Berlin. Only Nuncio Pacelli announced that he was staying at his post.

During the months since the Armistice, Pacelli had increased his efforts towards relief. In the embattled interim between the killing of Eisner and the proclamation of the Communist Government, he had continued to go about the city on errands of mercy, sometimes in his open touring car, often on foot. When he came to the barricades, manned by ragged, desperate men and women, he simply opened his cloak to show the golden jewelled pectoral cross on his breast and calmly climbed over them to continue on his way.

But the Bolshevists master-minding the mob knew that the Archbishop's unrelenting opposition to communism and his good works were as dangerous to them as the armed forces of the tottering democratic government in Berlin. No sooner had they seized the Bavarian Government than they started a campaign of hate against the Papal Nuncio. Returning one day from a visit to a poor quarter of the city,

Pacelli saw that the ground-floor windows of the Nunciature were shattered and its façade pock-marked by machine-gun bullets.

That very afternoon he heard a crash below stairs and raucous voices. Hurrying from his office, he saw that the hall was seething with an angry mob armed with everything from butcher knives to Luger automatics. Pacelli walked straight towards them. There was a sudden silence as they saw his tall, thin figure in black, with a violet sash around his waist and the gleaming cross on his breast.

"You must leave here," he said calmly. "This house does not belong to the Bavarian Government but to the Holy See. It is inviolable under international law."

There was a muttering rumble from the crowd and one of the leaders shouted, "What do we care for the Holy See? We'll leave if you show us your secret store of money and food."

"I have neither money nor food," said Pacelli simply. "For, as you know, I have given all I had to the poor of the city."

"That's a lie!" shouted the Communist.

"No, it's true," other voices cried. "Let us go."

Seeing that he was losing control of his band, the leader glared venomously and hurled his heavy automatic at the Archbishop. It struck him fair on the chest, denting the jewelled Cross. Pacelli put his hand to his breast, but continued to stand looking into the angry faces with eyes full of sorrow and pity.

Even the leader seemed shocked by what he had done. In an embarrassed silence the whole crowd shuffled out of the door.

Pacelli never knew the name of the man who had attacked him; nor why he threw the pistol instead of firing it. Perhaps it was out of ammunition, or perhaps some remnant of grace held him back from murdering a man who wore the livery of Christ. The Archbishop kept the badly bent Cross, and years later gave it to Francis Cardinal Spellman as a mark of his great affection.

Immediately after the attack on the Nunciature, Pacelli telephoned the Central Soviet of Munich to demand protection. All the satisfaction he got was a gruff voice saying, "You'd better get out of town!"

However good this advice might be, Pacelli had no intention of taking it. Nor did he propose to let danger keep him from going about his Master's business. Only a few days later, he went down to the Frauenplatz to confer with the Archbishop of Munich.

It was almost twilight when he started home, with a grey mist blowing off the River Isar. The streets were filled with sullen groups of men, glaring at the car. As it turned into the Maximilianstrasse along the embankment of the river, the groups coalesced into a mob, shouting threats and blasphemies. The car came to a dead stop, and the mob pressed against it, shaking it with their fury, threatening to overturn it. Inside, Pacelli said to his driver, "Put down the top."

The man looked at him as though he had gone mad, crying, *"Nein! Nein!"*

"Do as I say. Put it down."

The frightened driver, fumbling with the catches and straps, finally got the top down. The Archbishop stood up in the tonneau and then on the back seat so that even those at the farthest misty fringes of the crowd could see him. In his purple cloak, he was a shining target for any Communist with sufficient courage of his convictions to shoot.

None did. Instead a weird silence fell, and Pacelli's voice, high and clear, spoke to them: "My mission is peace," he said. "The only weapon I carry is this holy Cross. I do no harm to you, but only good things. Why should you harm me?"

Then raising his right hand in the immemorial gesture, he bestowed on them his blessing in the name of the Father, and of the Son and of the Holy Ghost.

There was not a sound from that great crowd as he sat down, and a lane opened magically for his car to pass on.

The forces of the Republican German Government under the command of General von Epp regained control of Munich in May 1919. His police immediately began hunting down the Reds. One of the first things they did was to call at the Nunciature to get information from Pacelli. But the Nuncio had no desire for revenge and would take no part in betraying his enemies. An apologetic secretary told the police commissioner, "His Excellency is at prayer. He cannot be disturbed."

When von Epp reported Pacelli's unco-operative attitude to his Chief, General von Ludendorff, the latter furiously remarked, "That isn't Christian behaviour; it's just a dirty trick!"

However, Pacelli repaid Ludendorff for his harsh words by helping to save him from being hauled before an Allied court for trial for 'war crimes'. Doubtless Ludendorff considered this 'Christian behaviour', which indeed it was.

In June, 1919, the new Bavarian assembly met and elected a democratic government. The danger of communism was over for the present. But in the beer halls of Munich a little group of malcontents was organising a new kind of subversive movement based on the seemingly fantastic dreams of an obscure Austrian corporal.

It had long been Pope Benedict's wish to have a Nuncio to all Germany. On a quick trip to Rome, Pacelli advised the Pope that the time was now propitious. Negotiations were begun, largely conducted by the Archbishop. They lasted almost a year. On June 30, 1920, Pacelli finally presented his credentials to President Ebert, as the first Apostolic Nuncio to the German Reich. At the same time the Archbishop also kept his status of Nuncio of Bavaria, and maintained his headquarters there, shuttling rapidly back and forth between Munich and Berlin.

It was a few months after this event that Pacelli received a very pleasant visit from his old friend Archbishop Achille Ratti.

Immediately on the formation of an independent Poland, Pope Benedict XV had appointed Ratti Apostolic Vicar, and later Nuncio, to Poland. Archbishop Ratti had not been long in Warsaw when Communist Russia declared war on Poland, and her vastly more numerous armies swept through the plains to the very gates of the Polish capital. As in Munich, most of the diplomats made a strategic retreat, but Ratti stayed on. He saw the new Polish citizens, worthy successors to the valiant Polish knights of old, break the Bolshevists on the banks of the Vistula and hurl them in a rout back across the Rusisan border. Now Ratti was going back to Rome to become Archbishop of Milan and a cardinal.

What the two old friends talked about those evenings in Munich is not known; but it is certainly a reasonable supposition that they agreed on the dangers of communism of which they had both seen the monstrous face at close quarters.

Archbishop Pacelli began at once the work of negotiating concordats with the German states. Pope Benedict would have liked to make a single agreement with all Germany, but this was impracticable under the Weimar Constitution, which made the German states semi-autonomous in such matters. The first step, then, was an agreement with predominantly Catholic Bavaria. The work of negotiation was interrupted on January 22, 1922, by the death of Benedict XV. Pacelli's personal grief at the loss of a friend was reinforced by his anxiety as to whether his successor would pursue the same policies. This worry vanished when on February 6, 1922, Achille Ratti was elected Pope and took the name of Pius XI.

The new Pope, who was widely travelled and had personally faced the problems of a new nation adjusting itself to freedom, was even more convinced than Benedict had been of the urgent necessity for concluding agreements with the new national entities such as Czechoslovakia and Yugoslavia, which had materialised from the Treaty of Versailles, and with the German States. With his full co-operation Archbishop Pacelli concluded the concordat with Bavaria.

Now was the time to move on to Berlin, for Prussia was the keystone of the whole German federal system, the biggest, richest and most powerful state. It was also mainly Protestant. If a concordat could be arranged with Prussia it would set the pattern for all Germany and possibly for other Protestant countries as well. In 1925, Archbishop Pacelli left Munich after seven years and moved his official residence to the German capital.

Despite the hazards and anxieties he had known in Munich, Pacelli had been deeply happy there. This paradox lies in his own nature, for it was there that he was able to serve people best—the lost, unhappy, starving little people of Germany. In doing so he was fulfilling the rôle he had hoped to play when he was young, the rôle of a simple priest, comforting and exhorting his flock, easing their earthly burdens, and gently leading them towards God.

When he moved on to Berlin, Pacelli took most of his Munich household with him. Among them was one who played a part which, though humble, is vastly important to the world.

When he first came to Munich, the new Nuncio called on the Prioress of the Franciscan Order at Altotting. In the course of their talk Pacelli asked, "Have you any sister who is capable of keeping house for me at the Nuncio's residence?"

The Prioress thought for some moments and then replied, "I could send you Sister Pasqualina. Of course she has been trained as a teacher, but she is very competent. Perhaps you would give her a trial."

So it was that Pacelli first met Sister—now Mother

Pasqualina. She is a small, sturdy, vivacious woman with bright kindly eyes that are lighted by humour and human understanding.

The trial of Mother Pasqualina is still going on. For forty years she has been in charge of Eugenio Pacelli's household, utterly untiring in her devotion to him. The Prioress did not exaggerate when she described Pasqualina as competent. In addition to her duties at the Vatican, Mother Pasqualina for years was head of Papal Relief Work in Germany. In her warehouse in the vaulted cellars beneath the Papal Palace, she processed all the pleas for help from that country by the light of a naked electric light bulb hanging from the high ceiling, and directed the despatch of needed supplies from the store of goods stacked all around her.

The Nunciature in Berlin was a fine big house surrounded by park-like grounds at Rauchstrasse 21. Pacelli had selected it, knowing that more diplomatic battles are won by entertaining than by writing notes. As soon as he was established there, the Archbishop began giving small informal parties to which the diplomatic and official worlds of Berlin flocked. President Ebert was a freqeunt guest, as were Chancellor Gustav Stresemann and most of his Cabinet, as well as Field-Marshal Paul von Hindenburg, who had laid aside his sword to become the elder statesman of democratic Germany. Nor were officials the only ones who came. Pacelli kept open house, and among his friends were students and aristocrats, workers and politicians.

For the same reasons, Pacelli set aside his preferred ascetic way of life, and began to go out a great deal. He soon became one of the best-known members of the diplomatic corps and was welcomed everywhere. Eminent Berliners from von Hindenburg himself to the American correspondent Dorothy Thompson acknowledged that he was "the best-informed diplomat in Germany."

Though he was working hard at negotiating the concordat, Pacelli did not confine his activities to that, but used his influence and oratory to promote peace and the welfare of the people throughout Germany. As early as 1923, when France invaded the Saar because Germany could not meet the staggering payments of reparations, Pacelli had been active in easing the war-like tensions that arose. Acting on his advice, Pope Pius XI had used all his influence to restrain the French Government from further inflammatory moves, and to induce them to get out of Germany. At the same time, when German resentment broke out in bombings and sabotage in the occupied territory, the Archbishop flew to the Saar in one of the early Lufthansa planes, and by his personal appeals to officials and to the Saarlanders, succeeded in abating the violence.

During his years in Berlin, he continued to travel up and down the land preaching sermons and making speeches. Whether he spoke in the pulpit or before a political audience his theme was always peace. He looked with horror on the rise of Nazism, and spoke his mind about it in no diplomatic terms. And always he urged the German people to forget the bitterness of war and defeat, and to work in friendship with their neighbours for the tranquillity of Europe.

It took four years of hard work and delicate manœuvres to negotiate the much desired Concordat. The 'Solemn Agreement', which was finally signed on June 24, 1929, allowed the Catholic Church to function in a country where Church and State had been recently separated. New dioceses could be set up and bishops elected and appointed, and the status of the Catholic clergy and their freedom to perform their duties were clearly defined. The delicate question of education was left out, but a gentleman's agreement with the German statesmen assured that the parochial schools could function without interference.

The treaty was ratified by the Reichstag on August 13, 1929. It was an amazing diplomatic achievement for Pacelli in the face of the rising tide of Nazism in a country where the *Kulturkampf* was becoming epitomised by atheism and, especially, by anti-Catholicism.

In November, 1929, Archbishop Pacelli went to Switzerland for a highly necessary rest. In the healing quiet of a narrow snow-filled valley below the sheer white peaks, he could at last enjoy complete solitude for prayer and meditation of which he had for so long been deprived. There the telegram from the Holy Father found him, announcing that he was to be elected a cardinal at the next consistory, and ordering him back to Rome.

Eugenio Pacelli was not elated at the prospect of becoming a Prince of the Church. He felt that his work in Germany was not yet done. Indeed, with the rise of what he later called 'the satanic spectre of Nazism', it was but just begun. He had told Pope Pius XI as much when he went to Rome to report on the signing of the Prussian Concordat. But the Holy Father in his wisdom had thought that there was a greater need in Rome, and had implied as much at the time.

The day after receiving the message, Archbishop Pacelli hurried back to Berlin to wind up the affairs of his embassy and accomplish what he could before leaving for Rome. The news of his approaching departure was received with real sorrow by his German friends. The Nunciature was thronged all day and part of the night by sentimental Germans saying good-bye with tears in their eyes.

General Paul von Hindenburg, now President of the German Republic, gave a farewell luncheon for the Nuncio. The grand old general, with his massive head and broad face, lined by age and wisdom, raised a glass and proposed a toast to Pacelli. His deep voice boomed down the long table as he said, "I thank you for all you have accomplished during these long years in the cause of peace, inspired as you have been by a high sense of justice and a deep love of humanity; and I can assure you that we shall not forget you and your work here."

To which Pacelli replied with a brief speech filled with his genuine affection for the German people and ending with the words, "My parting good wishes go out to the land and people entrusted to your rule."

The most touching scene of all came the day of the Nuncio's departure. It was evening when the Archbishop stepped into an open carriage provided by the German Government for his ride to the station. As the horses turned out of the park Pacelli could see that the Rauchstrasse was lined as far as his eyes could see with thousands upon thousands of people, many of them holding flaming torches high above their heads. As they saw him a great cheer broke out that thundered and roared on ahead of the slowly moving carriage.

Pacelli, with tears in his eyes, kept turning from right to left, giving his blessing to the people, many of whom knelt in the slushy street. He could not have helped but think of another misty evening in Munich when the crowd had cursed instead of cheering. But after all, they, too, had accepted his blessing.

The tremendous ovation extended all the way to the Anhalter Station, where the crowd was even more dense. Standing now in his carriage with the torchlight flickering on his tear-stained exalted face, Archbishop Pacelli gave his final blessing to the German people. However they might be misled in years to come, he always remembered the love they had shown him that evening, and he always believed that it was the true expression of their hearts.

*

CHAPTER NINE

THE RED HAT

THE journey from Berlin was long and tiring. The second morning after leaving the German capital, the train entered the Roman Campagna just as dawn was breaking over the hills around Rome. Pacelli wakened in response to a gentle knocking on the door of his compartment. A monsignor entered and, going over to the window, raised the blind and for a moment stood looking through the glass. Then, turning to the Archbishop, he said, "Look, Excellency, isn't it truly a paradise?"

The Nuncio did not answer, but let his gaze linger on the scene unfolding itself before him. Away in the east, the height of Monte Soratte was limned with gold as the sun climbed rapidly from behind it and made the dawn shadows retreat in soundless confusion over the waveless plain. The first light touched the umbrella pines and the cypresses, and the blackness of them became warm and gentle. As it lapped around the small farm houses their shuttered windows opened sleepy eyes, while the doves in a beating of wings flew into the sunburst. The first light reached the city, and the dome of St. Peter's revealed itself floating on a pearl-white mist. Behind it, the many spires and cross-crowned cupolas of Rome reached up to the sky.

The eyes of the Archbishop clouded with nostalgic memories as he looked on the city of his birth. He was coming home to his family from twelve years of exile, but his home was now sadly empty. His father was long dead, and his mother had died while he was in Bavaria. He knew that his sisters and his brother, Francesco, would be waiting for him.

His mind dwelt on Francesco and all that he had achieved and the success that had come to him. Like his father, Francesco had become a lawyer and had entered the service of the Church, rapidly reaching the first rank of his profession. He had been the Pope's legal adviser in the final settlement of the 'Roman Question', the political position of the temporal power of the Pope.

After 1870, when Italy was united in one kingdom and the Holy See lost its temporal domains, the Pope had shut himself up in the Vatican in a self-imposed imprisonment, in protest against the complete seizure of all the papal territory. As time went on, the Church realised that the lack of territory was, perhaps, not the great handicap it had once seemed. But it was necessary for the Pope to have some temporal dominion in order to exercise his functions as head of a universal church. He must be free and not be a citizen of, nor owe allegiance to, any one country, and he must manifestly appear as such. The Italian Government had continually shelved this question, and it was not until Mussolini became head of the Government and realised that the question must be solved sooner or later that anything was done.

Francesco was at this time legal counsellor to the Vatican. He was approached by Professor Barone, a Counsellor of State in the Italian Government. The first meeting was merely an exchange of views. Barone wished to find out on behalf of Mussolini, on what basis it would be possible to open negotiations. Francesco Pacelli conferred with Cardinal Gasparri, the then Secretary of State, and they decided that there were two main items—one was the establishment of a small sovereign state; and the other was the acknowledgement of the legal aspect of religious rites, particularly that of matrimony. The conversations went on until November, 1927, when Mussolini indicated that it was then possible to begin official negotiations. The King of Italy delegated Mussolini as head of the government, to conduct the affair, and the Pope gave Francesco Pacelli similar power.

It was not until February 11, 1929, that the pact was finally signed. The signing took place at noon in the Lateran Palace, hence its name, the Lateran Pact. Cardinal Gasparri set his name on the treaty on behalf of the Pope, and Mussolini on behalf of the Kingdom of Italy.

That morning Pius XI was giving a Lenten address to the parish priests of Rome and, as the clock struck twelve, he interrupted his sermon to announce what was taking place at that moment at the Lateran. This was the first official announcement, although everybody knew for some time that extraordinary events were shaping, and the wildest rumours had been afloat for many months.

Francesco had indeed worked hard and well, and Eugenio Pacelli, as he leaned back in the seat in his compartment, lingered with a fond pride over the fact that his brother had been instrumental in restoring to the Holy See some of its lost prestige. By this treaty the Holy See did not get back the territory over which it had ruled for more than a thousand years, and which had been stripped away almost overnight in 1870, but it was established as an independent sovereign state and received a money grant from the Italian Government for the lost territory. There were many clauses in the agreement, but substantially the Italian government acknowledged:

1. The Vatican City State was to be independent and sovereign, with the Pope its head, and with extra-territorial rights to certain property outside the boundaries of Vatican City. These were the major basilicas and various colleges, and the summer residence of the Popes at Castel Gandolfo.
2. The Pope's person was to be sacrosanct and inviolable.
3. The sole religion of the Italian State was to be Catholicism.
4. Religious instruction was given in both high school and any other school by ecclesiastics or by teachers with diocesan certificates.
5. Divorce was banned and the religious ceremony of matrimony was legally binding.
6. The seal of the confessional was to be legally acknowledged.
7. The Italian Government was to establish diplomatic relations with the new Vatican State.
8. Religious communities and orders were to have legal standing with the right to buy and sell and the right of private ownership.
9. The Holy See gave up all claim to the lost papal dominions.
10. The Holy See agreed to remain outside all temporal disputes between nations unless appealed to, but reserved the right to exercise its moral and spiritual power for the preservation of peace.

The Vatican City State now became an established fact, but the Holy See did not become a state, it merely possessed a state. It now had its own currency, police force, citizenship, diplomats and ambassadors, a small armed force, and its own flag of yellow and white. But one could not be of Vatican nationality. Even children born in the Vatican reverted, as a matter of course, to the nationality of their parents. People resident in the Vatican because of their office or of their work could receive Vatican citizenship, but only if their stay covered a lengthy period; and they would resume their own citizenship when they left.

Pacelli smiled to himself when he thought that on meeting his brother, he could call him 'Marquis'. For the Pope, in gratitude for all that Francesco Pacelli had done, had bestowed the title on him. But the Archbishop's eyes grew troubled again as he remembered the letter he had received asking him to return to Rome and informing him that he was to be created a cardinal. His experiences in Bavaria, and Germany, had made him aware that there was trouble ahead, and that as a cardinal and a diplomat the burden of the Cross would now be twice as heavy.

The train was now entering the suburbs of Rome, passing by sprawling *barrache* and utilitarian but ugly apartment blocks, and finally through the ancient Roman wall into the vast Termini Station. He descended from the carriage and faced the civic reception, walking slowly down the long line of carabinieri in their full-dress black uniforms, liberally laced with silver, wearing their long swords and their Napoleonic cockaded hats. He was driven swiftly to the Vatican, and officially announced his home-coming to the Holy See.

Once the official reception was over, while he was waiting for the College of Cardinals to meet and elect him a member, custom enjoined that Pacelli must wait elsewhere for the message to be brought to him. He chose the Palace of the Propaganda, in the Piazza di Spagna, for the few days at his disposal. He could not be present at the meeting of the Sacred College, which was held on December 16, 1929, for the cardinals gathered together as it were in secret, but in the evening a letter was brought to him at the Propaganda Palace. Beginning with his then title of 'Excellency', it informed him that His Holiness had been pleased to receive him into the College of Cardinals, and the letter ended with his new title of 'Eminence'. That was all; a simple letter conferred on him the honour of belonging to the élite group of princes of the Church. He murmured his thanks, but inwardly prayed that he might successfully carry out the extra duties that this new position would bring him.

Three days later, December 19, was the day fixed for conferring the outward sign of the cardinalate—the Red Hat. The ceremony was brief and not attended by any unnecessary pomp. The cardinals gathered in the Sistine Chapel, and Pacelli, flanked by two attendants, walked with hesitant steps to the foot of the altar and knelt before Pius XI. The folds of his silk mantle fell in a red circle around him and he held his head erect, as Pope Pius XI received the Hat from one of the servers and let it rest on his brow, pronouncing as he did so, "To the glory of Almighty God, receive this Red Hat, a sign of the cardinal's dignity. It signifies that you should be ready to shed your blood, if necessary, in the defence of the Holy Faith and for the preservation of peace among Christians. In the name of the Father, and of the Son, and of the Holy Ghost, Amen."

Pacelli rose from his knees and took his place among the cardinals. When the ceremony was over, the doors of the chapel were closed and another consistory or meeting was immediately held. This was not to discuss matters of moment, but to confer on the new cardinal the right of being able to speak and pronounce judgments in the future meetings of the Sacred College.

Again Pacelli knelt before Pius, and the Pope opened the mouth of the new cardinal and then closed it, signifying the right to speak. Pacelli then offered his right hand to the Pope and His Holiness placed on the fourth finger a gold ring, set with a large sapphire, the symbol of his office and of his authority.

All was over and the other cardinals welcomed their new colleague with congratulations, but Pacelli wished to go. As soon as he could, he left the Vatican and was driven home through the cold of the winter's evening.

As soon as a cardinal receives the Red Hat, he is appointed titular head of a church in Rome, whether he is Italian, British, American or any other nationality. Cardinal Pacelli was appointed to the Church of Saints John and Paul, one of the oldest in the city. It is a small but beautiful basilica which stands on the site of the Roman house where lived John and Paul, two patrician officers of the Roman Army in the final days of the Empire. In 360 A.D., when Emperor Julian the Apostate tried to undo the Christianising work of the great Constantine and ordered his people back to the darkness of paganism, John and Paul resigned their commissions, setting an example that infuriated the Emperor. He ordered their execution, but dared not do so publicly because of their great popularity. So a centurion with a squad of soldiers was sent to their home. As they were

D*

admitted the soldiers rushed the young patricians and, with sweeping strokes of their short swords, beheaded them.

When Rome again returned to the Christian faith, the house was turned into an oratory. Later the basilica was built near the place. In its gardens are the broken pillars and massive granite blocks of the Temple of Claudius, and under the crypt stand the ruined walls of the house of John and Paul, including the passageway in which rolled their severed heads.

On the morning of January 12, 1930, Eugenio Pacelli in his crimson robes climbed the ancient Roman street up the Coelian Hill, to take possession of his church. Though he had accepted his cardinalate with humble anxiety, he was beaming with pride in his beautiful little church which formed a link between the time when Christians were literally an underground movement, scurrying through the catacombs, and the emergence of Christianity as the almost universally accepted faith of the Western world.

As Cardinal Pacelli came into the small square on which his church fronted, Father Kierkels, head of the Passionist Order which serves the Church of Saints John and Paul, was waiting under its colonnaded entrance to receive him. The little procession entered the church and approached the high altar, where Cardinal Pacelli seated himself on the episcopal throne. As he listened gravely to Father Kierkel's address of welcome, the thin, classical outline of his face was as unemotional as marble, but his lively black eyes sparkling happily behind his spectacles gave him away.

When his turn came to reply, Pacelli spoke briefly of his pride in the fact that he was now head of a church with such a glorious history, which numbered saints among its

past leaders, and had been headed by no less than nine
Popes. He talked of the saints who lay buried there, "the
great apostle of the Crucified, St. Paul of the Cross, and the
lovely youthful, generous St. Gabriel of the Sorrowful
Mother, who wanted to picture Christ's sufferings on his
own body." Gravely, he hoped that he might be a little
worthy to follow in the footsteps of such glorious pre-
decessors.

Nor was he merely being sentimental. From that moment
until he was elected to the throne of St. Peter, Eugenio
Pacelli returned to his church to take part in its services as
often as he possibly could, and the Romans of the congregation felt that he was in truth their spiritual leader.

It is interesting to note that after Pacelli became Pope, he
appointed Francis Cardinal Spellman to head his best-loved
church.

The new cardinal was not given much time in which to
resume his duties as a priest. Pope Pius XI had brought him
back from Berlin for a definite purpose. On February 11,
Pietro Cardinal Gasparri, who had been re-appointed Secretary of State by Pius XI, asked permission to retire. He was
just over eighty years old, and now that the great works of
his life, the Lateran Pact, and the codification of Canon Law
were accomplished fact, he thought that he should hand
over his vast responsibilities to a younger man.

When Pius XI had first heard of his intention, he realised
that Pacelli was Gasparri's logical successor. The Pope knew
Pacelli well, both as a friend and a diplomat. Both had
faced the Communist terror that attacked central Europe
after World War I, Achille Ratti in Poland, and Pacelli in

Munich. They had worked together ever since with the same high purpose and like-minded methods. Pacelli's brilliant successes in his missions to Bavaria and Prussia, his wide knowledge of foreign affairs, and his record as a peace-maker, which some years later led Father Robert I. Gannon of Fordham University in New York to call him 'The Cardinal of Peace', were controlling considerations. In the letter of appointment which Pacelli received on February 10, 1930, the Pope wrote, "We make this appointment because of your spirit of piety and prayer; and also because of the great talents which God has given you."

There is no doubt Cardinal Pacelli was genuinely reluctant to accept this great office. He told his Pope and old friend he was not worthy. The Holy Father convinced him he must accept.

So, by the end of February, Pacelli found himself occupying the same office as the man who twenty years earlier had persuaded him to leave his pastoral work for the diplomatic field, and who had guided his first uncertain footsteps in that difficult arena. It is, of course, the most important post in the administration of the Church. The Secretary of State is the man who is nearest to the Holy Father. He is the only cardinal who lives in the Pope's part of the Vatican, and he is the guide and counsellor of His Holiness in both home and foreign policy. In fact, he is both Prime Minister and Foreign Secretary. All ambassadors and envoys to the Holy See are received by him in the name of the Pope, and it is he who repays the visits of statesmen and royalty to the Vatican.

In addition, he must keep in contact with all parts of the world, and have an encyclopædic knowledge of the affairs and problems of the Church and, indeed, of the governments in all the nations of the world.

When Pacelli entered the familiar office on the first morning, it was a little like coming home. Though it was vastly bigger than when he first came there, he spotted a young priest working hard at a crowded desk who might have been his youthful self; and he could put himself in the young man's place.

At the same time he was keenly aware that, despite the dedication of its members, the secretariat was like any other civil service. Its personnel could be trusted to perform their jobs safely without venturing any innovations in their filing systems, memo tablets or other routines. Though his staff was probably largely unaware of the changes in the political theories of the times, Pacelli was acutely conscious of them; and of the changes taking place in people themselves. He knew that he would have to grapple with problems presented by scientific advances and political retrogressions. The most ominous shadow on the picture was the rising popularity of totalitarianism—Fascist, Nazi and Communist. He was prepared to combat all three.

*

CHAPTER TEN

THE
STATESMAN-PRIEST

CARDINAL PACELLI had only been Secretary of State for a few days, when Cardinal Merry del Val suffered an attack of appendicitis, and died on the operating table. It was a deep blow to Eugenio Pacelli. For Merry del Val had been his close friend ever since their trip to England in 1908; and it seemed that another link with his youth had snapped. Some time later he delivered the eulogy at the unveiling of a monument to Cardinal Merry del Val. Expressing the fullness of his heart, he said, "During his entire life the beauty of his character shone forth in his many virtues, in his courageous confession of his faith, in his constancy, in his calm endurance, and, above all in his unswerving loyalty."

Pope Pius XI appointed Pacelli to succeed Merry del Val as Archpriest of St. Peter's. Thus, to his many duties as Secretary of State, Pacelli added the management of the largest Christian church in the world.

The great Basilica of St. Peter's stands on part of the ancient cemetery in which St. Peter was buried near the Circus of Emperor Nero, where thousands of early Christians were tortured for the enjoyment of the Emperor and the Roman rabble. St. Peter is said to have been crucified at the foot of the obelisk which stood in the Circus, and which was excavated by the orders of Pope Sixtus II in 1586, and placed in the centre of St. Peter's Square.

As early as 90 A.D., a small oratory was built over the spot. Constantine the Great destroyed the Circus and began the first basilica over St. Peter's tomb. On this same spot later rose the magnificent edifice, in part designed by Michelangelo and embellished by the greatest artists of the Renaissance, which is the very fount of the Catholic faith.

Cardinal Pacelli was very proud and diligent of his charge. True to his philosophy, he was most concerned about the *San Pietrini,* as are called the painters, cleaners, restorers and general repair men who belong to the corporation or guild charged with the care of St. Peter's ever since the sixteenth century and who spend their whole lives working in the Basilica. It is a jealously guarded guild, forming perhaps the most exclusive trade in the world. Membership is kept in the family, being handed down from father to son.

One day Pacelli was inspecting his church to see how the decorations for a forthcoming festival were going when, looking upward he saw a figure, tiny as a monkey, balancing on the very top of a ladder on a scaffolding in the awful height of Michelangelo's dome. Pacelli felt a sympathetic twitch of nerves. He threw up his hands in horror. "Get him down!" he commanded. "That is no place for a child!"

He watched anxiously as the minute creature crawled reluctantly down from that frightening perch. A few minutes later a small boy rushed up and planted himself firmly in front of the cardinal. "Please, Your Eminence," he said, "don't take my job away."

"How old are you, son?" Pacelli asked.

"I'm fifteen. I'm small for my age."

"That's much too young to be climbing about on ladders hundreds of feet in the air. It's impossible!"

Tear-dimmed brown eyes beseeched the cardinal. "My uncle is a San Pietrini," the boy said. "I must be one too, and one must learn young. Please, Father, let me!"

Pacelli, quite undone, could not hold to his resolution. "Very well," he said, "but please, please be careful!"

There was very little chance for the Cardinal-Secretary of State to indulge his fondness for children. However, on fine afternoons from four until five-fifteen, when his evening's work at the office began, he loved to go alone to the park of the Villa Borghese. After their siesta the children of Rome swarmed into the park to play under the shadow of its stately trees, watch the Punch and Judy show, and patronise the peanut vendors and the balloon men who moved around under an airborne pyramid of violently coloured bags of gas.

In the park Pacelli walked or read, his contemplations joyfully accompanied by the vibrant cries of young life all around him. Equally unperturbed by the tall figure of their friend, the children played tag around him or rushed to hide in the voluminous folds of his cassock. In quieter moments they took his hand and walked with him, talking gaily and offering tiny gifts, a piece of toffee or a burst balloon. When he left them Pacelli would sign the cross on their unlined foreheads.

ERRATUM

With reference to the matter covered on pages 101 and 102 it is desired to make the following correction:

Lord Strickland was not the British Governor but the Maltese Prime Minister; neither he, nor the British Governor, ever arrested an emissary of the Holy See. Lord Strickland was in fact a staunch Catholic.

When Pacelli became Secretary of State of the Holy See the world was at peace; and the prospect looked serene. The German Republic seemed firmly established, and Nazism was a minority party. The other nations of Europe were temporarily prosperous, and the general will to peace was exemplified by the signing of the pacts proposed by American Secretary of State Frank B. Kellogg in which most of the nations of the world renounced war as an instrument of policy. But there was something rotten under the fair surface, where the worm of totalitarianism burrowed deep.

The first serious problem with which Pacelli had to deal as Secretary of State was the matter of Malta. This vital little island fortress had been held by Saracens, Crusaders, Normans, Spaniards, French and British in turn. Its population was predominantly Catholic. In 1930, Malta was in turmoil. The British Governor, Lord Strickland, who was distinctly anti-Catholic, felt that some of his proposed reforms had been thwarted by the Archbishop of Malta, and he stirred up trouble.

The situation got even hotter when an emissary of the Holy See, sent to investigate conditions in Franciscan monasteries there, was arrested by the Governor. Protests from Pacelli were met by denunciations in the English papers of Catholic interference in the secular affairs of the island. The Colonial Office published a 'Blue Book' setting forth Lord Strickland's version of the affair.

The Pope asked his Secretary of State personally to discover the truth of the matter. In doing so Pacelli examined all the documents in the case and questioned witnesses from Malta. His conclusions were published in a 'White Paper' on June 22, 1930.

Pacelli's statement seemed so eminently fair and temperate that the British Government sent a Royal Commission to the island to make its own investigation. The report of the commission completely confirmed that of Pacelli. Lord Strickland was ordered by his government to apologise to the Archbishop of Malta and the Holy See.

This diplomatic victory established Pacelli's reputation in the chancelleries of Europe. But far more important was the fact that it was not obtained by pressure or conniving, but by simply telling the truth. Because this was so, and because the British Government generously acknowledged its error, it was one of the few diplomatic triumphs that made everybody happy—except, of course, Lord Strickland.

The Malta matter was a minor thing compared to the troubles that developed in Italy. The Pope and his advisers had thought that the signing of the Lateran Pact would at long last produce an era of good feeling between the Church and the Government of Italy. But it is the nature of totalitarian governments that they must be *total*. Mussolini soon set out to increase his area of totality.

The Duce began by announcing quite cynically in the Italian Parliament that he proposed to use the Church to gain his own ends. Soon after that the Fascist authorities moved in on education and especially youth clubs and youth organisations. Pius XI was enthusiastically supporting Catholic Action, a non-political organisation that tried to encourage lay members of the Church to take part in parish affairs. Its principal activity was the establishment of youth clubs, playrooms, sports and educational facilities in each parish.

From Mussolini's point of view this was dangerously sub-

versive. He knew he had to mould the minds of Italian
youth or perish. So secret orders went out to incite gangs of
Blackshirt juvenile delinquents to attack the Catholic Youth
Clubs. When the members defended themselves, several of
the clubs were closed for "disturbing the public peace".
Individuals and groups of Catholic Action members were
mobbed and stoned in the streets. This, of course, did not
disturb the peace.

Pacelli protested violently to Mussolini, who retorted by
accusing the Catholic Action groups of political activities.
With the whole mechanism of the Italian State, including
the courts, in Mussolini's grip, the position of the Holy See
appeared to be hopeless. But Pacelli had a trick or two up
the sleeves of his cassock.

The only way to combat the Fascists was by the pressure
of world opinion. Pacelli advised his Pope to prepare an
encyclical. With the assistance of his Secretary of State, His
Holiness wrote a forthright statement describing Fascist
methods; their acts of oppression, their efforts at terrorism
and their protection racket. But the question remained, how
to publish it?

For the Pope was more truly a prisoner of the Vatican
than when he had been so by his own choosing. Fascist
guards ringed Vatican City, and Mussolini controlled the
whole Italian press. If Pacelli attempted to release the
encyclical to the Italian papers it would be suppressed
immediately. Even if he delivered it to the foreign news
correspondents, their cables would be delayed and muti-
lated by censorship. Since the Fascists also controlled the
telephones and censored the mails, it was impossible to communicate it direct to foreign countries.

At this point Pacelli called into his office an energetic young American monsignor who was attached to the Secretariat. He handed the encyclical to him and said, "You are to smuggle this to Paris, and give it to the world press. Don't waste a moment, and don't get caught."

Monsignor Francis J. Spellman acted in the best traditions of cloak-and-dagger diplomacy. He piled into a small, unmarked automobile and was driven direct to the airport. There he stepped aboard the first plane to Paris. The moment it touched down at Le Bourget, Spellman handed the encyclical to the reporters. The first Mussolini heard about it was when it was telephoned back to the Roman papers.

The Duce was no fool. He realised now that Pacelli was too astute a diplomat to be ignored. The encyclical was published on June 29, 1931. In August Mussolini indicated that he was ready to discuss the matter reasonably. And in September he and Pacelli signed an agreement. It was brief, but explicit. The scope of Catholic Action was clearly defined, and its freedom to operate was guaranteed.

However, Pacelli was determined never to get in a spot like that again. With Pius's approval, he got Guglielmo Marconi himself to install a radio station in Vatican City, by which the Pope could communicate with all the world. In addition, Pacelli proceeded to streamline the Vatican. Sleek American automobiles replaced its venerable carriages; an electric power plant was built; lifts were installed, and there was even a telephoto sending apparatus. A modern secretary must have modern equipment.

Pacelli soon had need of it. Touched off by the great depression in America, the economic position of Europe began to deteriorate; and, as country after country felt the pinch, the whole façade of world serenity cracked and crumbled. Germany fell into the totalitarian clutches of Hitler. Civil war broke out in Spain, while France teetered on the verge of a state socialism with strong totalitarian tendencies. From behind the impenetrable walls of the Kremlin the atheistic masters of Russia malevolently exploited every area of human misery for the purpose of their crusade against the Cross.

So troubles fell thick upon Pacelli's head. The Holy See recognised the Spanish Republic. Then, as radicals got control of the Spanish Government, it turned against the Church; and in the Communist districts atrocities were committed against the clergy. In Mexico, the left wing government was strongly anti-clerical and imposed crippling legal restrictions against the Church. Nazi Germany, demanding total mental submission of its subjects, fought against any god but Hitler. And everywhere the Communists backed anti-Christ, whatever alias he wore.

Pope Pius and Pacelli could do little to combat these attacks in a physical sense. There were no economic pressures they could bring to bear, and little in the way of diplomatic influence. All they could do was to advise the Catholic clergy to keep cool, and not give the enemies of the Church any excuse for violent action. Beyond that they relied on the moral power of faith, which sometimes works slowly, but triumphs in the end.

Indeed, Pacelli went so far as to negotiate a new concordat with Hitler's government, establishing the rights and religious freedom of the Catholic minority in Germany—needless to say its terms were violated. In addition, concordats were negotiated with Catholic Austria and Yugoslavia.

It is impossible to say definitely who was responsible for which aspect of Vatican policy during this troubled decade, Pope Pius XI or his Secretary of State, for the two worked so closely together that there is no evidence of any difference of opinion between them. Indeed, the Holy Father once said, "Cardinal Pacelli speaks with my voice."

Yet never were two co-workers less alike. Achille Ratti was small and heavy; slow in his movements, with a hard will. He was like a dormant volcano, slow to erupt, but capable of violent bursts of energy. Pacelli was tall and slim, as quick and versatile as a chameleon, and as lively as the dancing blue flame of a turf fire. But their opposite qualities produced *apposition* between them. They supplemented each other. And they were true friends.

Not all of Pacelli's days as Secretary of State were toilsome and harassed. There were happy occasions, and moments of great triumph. Such was his trip to Argentine as Papel Legate to the Eucharistic Congress held in Buenos Aires in 1934, when the faithful of all the world gathered to honour Christ the King in the Sacrament of the Eucharist. These congresses are held in a different world capital each time. It was many years since Pacelli had attended the one in London in a minor capacity.

The Cardinal-Secretary of State slipped out of Rome on the evening of September 24. There was no official departure ceremony, and he expected to board his ship at Genoa as quietly. But when the train rumbled into the Genoa station next morning, cheering crowds jammed the platform. Pacelli was escorted to the Archbishop's palace, where he said Mass. Then he proceeded to the port.

The way led through densely crowded streets, with every church bell clanging in voices of bronze and silver, and the people shouting, "God speed!"

As soon as the Papal mission boarded the *Conte Grande,* she got under way and steamed out of the harbour while shrilling whistles drowned the singing bells.

Aboard ship, Pacelli spent most of his time brushing up his Spanish. They crossed the equator on October 1, but this time the traditional ceremony to King Neptune was replaced by one to Christ the King. Standing amid the instruments of navigation on the bridge, with the wind blowing his scarlet robes, the cardinal held the Benediction service and raising the Consecrated Host on high blessed the immensity of the ocean.

Pacelli remained on the bridge while the sea turned from gold to purple in the sunset, waiting to see the Southern Cross. When at last it glittered above the forecastle, he spoke of the time, sixteen centuries before, when the cross of stars appeared to the Emperor Constantine over the Ponte Milvio in Rome, and a Voice said, "In this Sign you shall conquer."

As the *Conte Grande* sailed into the Plata River, everybody and everything in Buenos Aires seemed to be out to welcome her. There were aeroplanes overhead, dipping and rolling. Battleships, cruisers and destroyers of the Argentine Navy foamed down the river—the *25th Mayo, Almirante Brown, Mindoza, Tucuman, Lariopa,* and *Garay.* As the cardinal appeared on the bridge with the sunlight brilliant on the Roman purple of his mantle, the warships formed up around the *Conte Grande,* firing a royal salute, and the yellow and white Papal flag broke out from their mastheads.

Nearer the city the welcome became frenzied. The wide river was jammed with every conceivable kind of craft—yachts, excursion steamers, sailing boats, barges, rowing boats, and even dugout canoes, all of them decorated with the Papal colours. As the ship nosed into the basin, the battery at the entrance fired a salute, but the sharp crack of the guns was all but lost in the bellowing, shrieking, tooting whistles and the crashing cheers of half a million people. Pacelli's eyes were bright with triumph, but not for himself. Those standing close heard him exclaim, "A magnificent welcome for Christ the King."

Argentina gave its all to celebrate the congress with unparalleled splendour. The President, General Augusto Justo, led the worshippers in public functions and private services as well. The day devoted to the children was blinding as 107,000 youngsters dressed entirely in white took their places before the outdoor altar in the blazing sunshine to sing their hymns of praise and adoration.

The final day culminated in a service in Palermo Park, where the President dedicated the Republic to Christ the King. Followed by five other cardinals and eighty mitred bishops, Pacelli ascended the altar for the Pontifical Mass. During the ceremonies he spoke to the people for over an hour in fluent Spanish. Mincing no words, he described the disorders affecting the world and condemned the new ideologies that were arising with their denial of honesty and morality. And he spoke of the need for peace, the peace of Christ.

"But," he concluded, "it is greatly consoling that in this new courtroom of the world Christ does not stand alone as he did in Pilate's court. At His side now stand many devoted souls, for at His side stands the Church. And the more grimly and fiercely the clamour of godlessness arises against Him, the more fervently we proclaim Him the immortal King of all times."

There followed the procession of the Eucharist. On a carriage covered with gay tropical flowers and drawn by priests in white surplices and stoles, the Sacrament was carried high. Behind it knelt the figure of the cardinal. For two hours he rode thus, kneeling motionless, his hands joined together and resting on the altar, his eyes fixed in adoration on the Host above his head, while the procession slowly moved through mile after mile of streets filled with kneeling people.

On the way home the *Conte Grande* stopped at Rio de Janeiro, where Pacelli was received in state by the Parliament and the Supreme Court, both of which he addressed in Portuguese. Then back along the long sunny sea miles to Rome; and to the darkening clouds of the Abyssinian war.

The night after Pacelli reached Rome, a telegram was delivered to him. Thinking it too important to wait, his secretary went to the cardinal's room, even though it was very late. He knocked and slipped quietly through the unlocked door. The room was dark, but in the dim light from the windows the secretary's startled eyes saw a tall figure hoist itself from the marble floor.

As the lights came on, the cardinal took the telegram from his secretary and, seeing his agitation, smilingly said, "Do not be worried. After so much glory and splendour, it is necessary to lie close to the earth to know that we are nothing."

*

CHAPTER ELEVEN

"HEY, MISTER CARDINAL!"

ON his return from Argentina, Pacelli was plunged into a fresh crisis; Italy was bubbling with war fever as Mussolini's imagination pursued the phantasy of the New Roman Empire. With all the vast propaganda power of a controlled press he incited the people to war against Ethiopia. Small incursions and clashes occurring on the Italo-Abyssinian border in Africa were used as a pretext for the attack on what the Duce planned as the first province of his new empire.

Pacelli was horrified by the preparations for war that he saw going gaily forward. Though the Lateran Pact excluded the Pope from direct interference with Italian policy, it did not prevent his speaking his mind. The burning anger of Pacelli could be heard in the voice of Pope Pius XI as he condemned the proposed aggression as, "A crime so enormous, a manifestation of such mad folly, that We hold it to be absolutely impossible."

In Germany, too, trouble was piling up. The solemn concordat signed by Pacelli for the Holy See and by Vice-Chancellor von Papen for Hitler meant nothing to the Nazi dictator. Hitler started a deliberate campaign to extirpate the Catholic Church from the Reich. All Catholic political parties were dissolved; Catholic organisations, social clubs and youth clubs were disbanded. The German press was more tightly muzzled than the Italian papers, but the Holy See fought back from pulpits everywhere. In the Vatican City newspaper and over the Vatican radio, the Holy See denounced this neo-paganism calling it, "The cult of force, the oppressors of the freedom and dignity of man."

Pacelli wrote an open letter to Cardinal Schulte, Archbishop of Cologne, calling on the hierarchy and clergy of Germany to fight the menace of Hitlerism: "When the Holy Church and the Supreme Pontiff are made the targets of outrageous attacks, when the lying attempt is made to trump up an antagonism between loyalty to the Church and loyalty to the earthly fatherland, then the hour is struck when the bishop must raise his voice and fearlessly repeat the words of the Apostle, 'Whether it be right to hearken unto you, more than to God.'"

In the middle of all this turbulence, in April 1935, Pacelli was sent to Lourdes in the south of France. At this most renowned shrine to the Mother of the Saviour pilgrims of all nations were gathered to pray in all tongues for the preservation of the peace of the world.

Eugenio Pacelli went with sorrow in his heart; for two days previously Francesco had died. The cardinal had been bound by very intimate ties to his older brother; and, as the train jerked around the violent curves of its Alpine route, he thought of the days when as a little boy he used to wait for the comforting protection of Francesco's hand to see him safely home from school.

On the last of the three days of prayer at Lourdes, Cardinal Pacelli, assisted by Cardinal van Rotey and Luigi Maglione,

the Apostolic Nuncio to Paris, celebrated pontifical Mass in
the famous grotto in the foothills of the Pyrenees. His voice,
cold and clear as the mountain torrent by which he stood,
once more condemned the modern pagan ideas of racism and
totalitarianism: "What is tragic is that this aversion to the
Cross is increased to the utmost by those who deny the fun-
damental dogma of sin and reject the idea of redemption as
injurious to human dignity. With the illusion of extolling
new wisdom, they are only lamentable plagiarists who cover
old errors with new trumpery. It matters little that they
mass around the flag of social revolution. They are inspired
by a false conception of the world and life. Whether they
are possessed by superstitions of race and blood or by false
conceptions of the social and economic world, their philosophy is essentially opposed to the Christian faith. And on
such principles the Church does not consent to form a com-
pact with them at any price."

Ever since his invitation to become a professor at the
Catholic University in Washington, Eugenio Pacelli had
wanted to go to America. In this he was like most Europeans,
rich and poor, intellectual and ignorant, whose dearest wish
was to go to that—in Europe—fabled land. In 1936 Pacelli's
chance came. He recognised that the aggressions of totalita-
rians, of the Right and Left alike, were part of a world-wide
attack on the Catholic Church. And he proposed not to
choose between either of these monsters, but to rely on
strengthening the solidarity of Catholics throughout the
world. In line with this policy and to make contacts in the
United States, which had no diplomatic ties with the Vatican,
he asked the Holy Father's permission to make the trip.

The ageing Pope replied, *"Va figliolo, staccati un instante da me. Viaggia!"*—"Go, little son, leave me for a short time. Travel!"

Pius XI could ill spare his right hand man at such a time of turbulence, but he was convinced of the value of Pacelli's mission, and the importance to his Secretary of State of a first-hand knowledge of all the world.

Pacelli sailed from Naples in the fast new liner, *Conte di Savoia,* early in October. This was the first time in history that a Papal Secretary of State had visited the United States. As the ship lay to in the Narrows of New York Harbour, a tremendous crowd of reporters swarmed aboard. Pacelli was literally mobbed and swamped by shouted questions. One photographer climbed up on a life boat, where he had a fine view of the back of Pacelli's head. "Hey, Mister Cardinal!" he yelled. "Look this way."

Laughing, his Eminence complied.

Pacelli had, in fact, been well briefed on the ways of American journalists, and on the way over he had typed out a "handout" himself, which he now distributed to the reporters. In it he emphasised that his visit was purely personal—to see for himself the country "where people know how to unite so nobly a sense of discipline with a well-ordered liberty."

The crowding, pushing reporters, the colloquial questioning, and the lightning storm of flashbulbs did not bother him at all. Smiling happily, he walked down the gangway determined to see America like an American.

So he did all the things a tourist is supposed to do. He shot up to the top of the Empire State Building, and properly admired the skyline of New York. In Philadelphia, he saw the Liberty Bell, and in Washington drove out to Mount Vernon. He thought that ride behind the screaming motor-cycles of his escorts was great fun, for he always loved speed.

In Washington, he gave an address at the Catholic University, where he spoke a little wistfully of its offer of a professorship, saying, "Only the fatherly prohibition of Pius X kept me from accepting such an agreeable invitation, and so it does not seem to be entirely strange that I am here."

During his stay in the capital he made his only political speech—if you could call it that—to five hundred newspaper-men at a luncheon in his honour at the National Press Club. Speaking his slow, precise English, he told them of their responsibilities for moulding public opinion towards peace, and added, "Glory belongs not only to those who triumph on the battlefield, but to those who safeguard tranquillity and peace."

Then the cardinal chartered an aeroplane, and roared away on a whirlwind tour of the United States: Cleveland, Chicago, Notre Dame—where he received an honorary degree—St. Paul, San Francisco, Los Angeles and Hollywood—where he enjoyed a visit to a movie studio—Boulder Dam, Kansas City, and back to Chicago. Though he visited many Catholic institutions, he did not confine his interests to them, but endeavoured to make contact with every aspect of American life.

The Cardinal used his plane as an office, and had his portable typewriter set up on a table in front of his chair so that he could write letters and speeches in flight. At Chicago the plane ran into bad weather and had to circle the field for over an hour. Worried airline officials greeted Pacelli with profuse regrets when it finally landed.

The cardinal laughingly said, "No apologies, gentlemen! I ought to thank you for giving me a little time to catch up on my reading."

On his way back to New York, Pacelli stopped for a last typical tourist sight—Niagara Falls. He stood silently for long minutes on the brink, looking down at the glorious, glistening rush of water crashing down into rainbow spray. Then he turned to go, turned back, and with a spontaneous gesture blessed the Falls.

In New York, the cardinal stayed most of the time with Mrs. Nicholas Brady at her lovely Long Island estate. Mrs. Brady had been created a Papal duchess for her great service to the Church, but she never used her title in America. In Europe, however, she was known as Duchess Brady. Pacelli also spent a night or two in New York City with Myron Taylor, who much later became President Roosevelt's unofficial envoy to the Vatican.

Pacelli was an extremely clever diplomat, and his knowledge of history told him how very touchy Americans were about outside interference with national politics. With President Roosevelt running for re-election, the cardinal had carefully refrained from seeing him so that everyone could be certain that he was not favouring either candidate. After Roosevelt was re-elected, Pacelli accepted an invitation to lunch at Hyde Park.

On the last day of his stay in the United States, Pacelli motored up the parkways to Hyde Park through a brilliance of foliage such as he had never seen. The old frame house on the Hudson, with its pillared portico in front, and its ramshackle Victorian veranda at the back overlooking the splendid sweep of the river, must have seemed an extraordinarily simple place for so great a ruler to live to a man who came from Italy, where almost everybody of any importance—and many people of none at all—lives in palaces. However, the President and Mrs. Roosevelt gave their home a warm and welcoming quality which Pacelli fully appreciated. As Roosevelt himself would have put it, the President and the cardinal 'hit it off'.

When he came out of the front door, Pacelli was charged by the White House correspondents, who day and night hang around the President's residence hungrily snapping up crumbs of news. In answer to their vociferous questions, the diplomatic prelate would only say, "I enjoyed lunching with a typical American family," which description of the Roosevelts was either touchingly naïve or remarkably subtle.

As he boarded the ship for his return voyage, Pacelli said with real sincerity, "I am leaving America with sorrow, and yet with gratitude in my heart to all with whom I have come in contact, and with the prayer that Almighty God may continue to bless this great nation, that its citizens may be happy, and that the influence of the United States may continue to be exercised for the promotion of peace among peoples."

Looking back on his trip, Eugenio Pacelli could feel that it had been well worth while. He had covered 16,000 miles, and had attended innumerable conferences, receptions, religious ceremonies, and public functions of all kinds. More important still, he had spent hours with Americans in their homes, getting to know them, helping them to know the aspirations and policies of the Catholic Church. He had felt at home in America and had begun many lasting friend-

At fifteen, Eugenio Pacelli entered the Liceo Quirini Visconti to complete his secondary schooling before entering Capranica College in 1894.

Attualità Giordani

The Swiss Guards, known as the Army of the Vatican, are seen here on parade wearing their armour and bearing their traditional halberds.

Attualità Giordani

In 1917, Pius XII was named Papal Nuncio to Bavaria. Three years later after being elevated to Archbishop of Sardes he was named Papal Nuncio to all of Germany. Here he is shown talking to German army men in Bavaria.

In the Square of Heroes at Budapest, Cardinal Pacelli warned the world that Communism had raised its "clenched

The interior of St. Peter's, decorated especially for the coronation ceremonies by the San Pietrini, was a quiet combination of reds, whites and yellows. With members of the College of Cardinals seated in the foreground, the simple white Papal throne is seen below the Chair of St. Peter.

G. Felici

Elected by the Consistory of Cardinals on March 2, 1939, Pius XII
was crowned Pope ten days later. Here he is seen on the throne in
St. Peter's.

Crowned with the Tiara, Pius descended the podium and walked to the balustrade. His voice rang out across the Square, clear and strong: "May the blessing of Almighty God, Father, Son and Holy Ghost descend upon you, and remain with you forever!"

Pius XII during a service in the beautiful Sistine Chapel.

On a hot May day, Pius XII was enthroned as Bishop of Rome, the enthroning taking place in the Basilica of St. John Lateran, titular church of the Bishop of Rome, to which Pius is here seen being carried.

Attualità Giordani

On the morning of July 19, 1943, Rome was bombed from the air for the first time. Drawing money from the Vatican Bank, Pius XII rushed to the scene of the damage to bring relief to the bombed out.

Attualità Giordani

On August 13, Rome was raided again. Heedless of falling masonry, the Pope went to the San Giovanni district and ministered to the wounded in front of the Church of St. John Lateran, unaware his shoes were cut by broken glass and his clothing and hands smeared with blood.

Attualità Giordani

For the first time since before the fall of Rome in 1870 a Pope was crowned in public. Here the senior cardinal-deacon places the triple crown upon the head of Pius XII before the eyes of a throng so great no one could guess its number.

Attualità Giordani

In December, 1948, the Communist regime of Hungary arrested Cardinal Mindzenty. The people of the world protested and Pius XII, from the balcony of St. Peter's, voiced his protest to a great throng which had gathered below.

Toward the end of the Holy Year—on November 1, 1950—the
Pope proclaimed the Dogma of the Assumption of the Virgin,
officially confirming a belief long held.

Il Messaggero

The Pope's apartment is always filled with song, supplied by four cages of birds. Here he is shown with his favourite, a goldfinch named Gretel.

Attualità Giordani

In 1951, Pius XII celebrated the beatification of Pope Pius X who three years later was canonised in a cere-

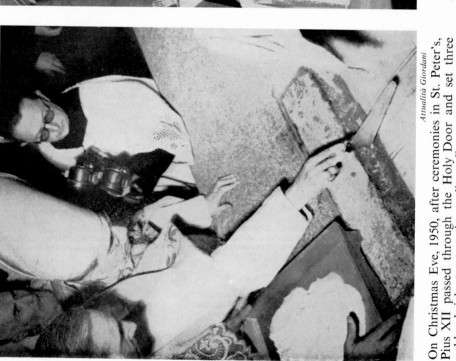

Attualità Giordani

On Christmas Eve, 1950, after ceremonies in St. Peter's, Pius XII passed through the Holy Door and set three golden bricks to start the sealing-off process so that the

ships. His personal contact with President Roosevelt was alone enough to justify the trip, since in the confused days of war it was to result in closer co-operation between the Holy See and the American Government than had ever been known before.

The Cardinal's arrival in Rome was an unhappy return to cold realities. Pope Pius XI was very ill. Pacelli had been appointed Camerlengo of the Church in 1935, which meant that if the Holy Father died he must make all executive decisions until a Conclave met and a new Pope was elected. Thus, in addition to anxiety for his beloved Pope, were added mounting cares of state.

In December, 1936, Europe presented a dismal contrast to the comparatively tranquil American scene. The Civil War in Spain was being used as a proving ground where the rival ideologies were trying out new weapons and testing their strength. On the one hand the radical Republican Government was backed by Russia, which saw an opportunity for spreading Communist doctrine in Europe. General Franco's 'Rebels' were being helped by the German and Italian dictators for similar reasons. The Holy See at first could take no sides in such a struggle, but as the Reds became paramount in the Republican Government, persecutions against Catholics broke out. Massacres, burnings, pillagings and unspeakable atrocities were committed against Catholics.

The Pope, lying racked by the agonies of a damaged heart, could only offer his sufferings as a sacrifice "for the peace and goodwill of the Church and the whole world."

Pacelli was torn to see his friend and master succumbing to this mental and physical anguish. But he could do nothing to stop the stampede of events as the Spanish war intensified into an ever more ruthless struggle between the totalitarian camps.

The Cardinal-Secretary of State was also concerned by the danger of the growing solidarity between Hitler and Mussolini. The Duce, envious of Hitler's successes in acquiring territory and power, decided to imitate some of his policies, just as in the beginning, Hitler had imitated him. The Fascists added anti-semitism to their cult and began to try to inculcate it among the Italian people. At the same time Hitler was beguiling Mussolini with avowals of eternal friendship for Italy.

Pacelli was acutely aware of the falsity of such protestation, and set out to uncover factual material for an exposé of Nazism. These facts were embodied in the encyclical published by Pius XI in German on March 19, 1937, which forthrightly condemned the whole Hitler régime and the anti-Christian policy of the Nazis, citing details, dates and places, and outlining the methods used to exterminate religion in the Reich.

That brought on the first fuming visit of the German Ambassador to the Vatican, Herr Doktor von Bergen, who protested violently and demanded retraction. Cardinal Pacelli replied that there could be no retraction of the truth.

Four weeks later von Bergen was back again, positively apoplectic. It seemed that George Cardinal Mundelein of Chicago had had the temerity to make a speech in Chicago attacking Nazism, Hitler, Goering, Goebbels and the rest of their crew for persecution of religion, and vehemently denouncing the whole pattern of events in Germany.

Pacelli listened impassively to von Bergen's lamentations, and to his demands that something be done about this 'atrocious offence'. When the Nazi Ambassador finished, the smiling cardinal sauvely replied, "We are neither willing, nor are we able to restrict the freedom of speech of an American citizen who wishes to expose the falsities of a foreign government. Freedom of speech is an American birthright."

*

CHAPTER TWELVE

THE

PASSING OF A POPE

CARDINAL PACELLI's travels continued in 1937 with another
trip to France to attend ceremonies at Lisieux in Normandy,
where a new basilica to St. Thérèse of Lisieux was to be
dedicated. Once again he was making history because, until
Pacelli, no Papal Legate since 1814 had been officially welcomed by the French Government.

At the Gare de Lyon a deputation headed by the Prime
Minister of France and the Minister of Foreign Affairs was
waiting to receive him in state. Pacelli walked between the
ranks of the magnificently accoutred *Garde Républicaine,*
who stood to attention with the French Tricolour and the
Papal flag side by side. Beyond the barriers a great crowd
cheered as Pacelli, in his scarlet cape with the golden pectoral
cross on his breast, and carrying his black, red-corded hat,
greeted the officials. There is no doubt that the French
people loved him, for his personality and poise commended
him to a nation which prides itself on its elegance and
civilised way of life. They saw in him a man whose intelligence and bearing they could understand and respect.

After the ceremonies at Lisieux, Pacelli preached a sermon in the great Gothic cathedral of Notre Dame de Paris. As he mounted to the high pulpit from which so many renowned prelates had spoken, he saw a great company gathered under the soaring, pointed arches of the nave. President Le Brun of France was there, surrounded by his cabinet. The high judges of the law courts, marshals of France, admirals, and representatives of the famous universities and of every aspect of French life were in the company.

Pacelli talked to them simply in fluent French. To the intellectuals and atheists among them, as well as to the faithful, he said plainly, "The sooner everyone fully realises that there is a definite correlation between the mission of the Church of Christ and the progress and greatness of nations, the sooner will come the harmony which God desires."

On the train home Pacelli worked as always on pressing Vatican business. When he had disposed of it, he drew from his brief-case a small book bound in black leather with many ribbon book-markers and read the office of the day. Again, as he had many times before, he came across the psalm which had been his favourite for more than forty years: "All flesh is grass and glory passes like the flowers of the field."

Early in 1938, the forces of 'militant godlessness', as Pacelli called them, began to march. Hitler took Austria, and imposed *Anschluss* on its people, incorporating them into the Reich. At the first movement of Nazi troops towards the Austrian border, Pacelli sent for the Papal Nuncio to the

Italian Government and conferred on the advisability of asking Mussolini to save Austrian independence. In 1934, a similar move by Hitler had been stopped in its tracks by the Duce's "No!"

But this time it was hopeless. The dictators had moved closer together, and were now hand in glove. Matters were worsened when Theodore Cardinal Innitzer, Archibshop of Vienna, advised the Austrian Catholics to vote in the plebiscite for *Anschluss*.

The Vatican radio immediately broadcast a vehement denunciation of this suggestion, and Pacelli ordered the cardinal to Rome, where he dressed that dignitary down like an admiral reprimanding a midshipman. Innitzer was ordered to sign a retraction of his statement.

A month later Pacelli made the last of his many voyages. He went as Papal Legate to the International Eucharistic Congress in Budapest. Admiral Horthy, Regent of Hungary, invited him to be his guest at the Royal Castle.

On this trip Pacelli astonished even his own intimates by his furious energy and will power. In the short time at his disposal he actually learned enough Hungarian to be able to talk to the wildly enthusiastic people, as well as to address many meetings and conferences. On the last day Pacelli celebrated Pontifical Mass, assisted by thirteen cardinals and no less than two hundred and fifty bishops.

The Eucharistic procession was held on the Danube. It was dusk when the procession started, and the banks of that romantic river were lined by thousands of people holding torches and lighted candles. The Sacred Host was carried on a barge, whose jewelled decorations reflected the wavering light of the myriad *flambeaux* on the shore. Motionless, as though carved of red porphyry, the cardinal knelt before the Presence, his eye fixed beseechingly on the Monstrance.

Later, standing underneath a splendid canopy supported by four tall, twisted columns in the Square of Heroes, Pacelli made his last and most moving address to the people of a foreign land. "Lined up against us," he said, "is a new, sad front of fighters—fighters without God, who raise their clenched fists of anti-Christ in menacing defiance against heaven and everything that is sacred to us. The leaders of atheistic communism are trying to blanket the earth with a violent revolution. Nations threatened by this danger have a right to oppose it. True, we cannot praise highly enough the superhuman efforts of the statesmen who do their utmost through education and strong government to check these disturbers of social peace. . . . But all these efforts to stave off this calamity will be fruitless unless the spirit of justice and love enters again into the hearts of men and unites them in brotherly love.

"The eyes of the divine Saviour search our eyes. His lips beseech us, repeating once again His immortal words: 'This, my commandment, I give unto you, that you love one another as I have loved you.'"

The cardinal made his way wearily homeward, dreading to face the problems that waited in his small office off the Square of St. Damaso. The hardest of these was the fact that Pius XI had never fully recovered from his heart attack. To personal sorrow was added that fact that most of the government of the Church had fallen on Pacelli's shoulders.

Meanwhile, Hitler was doing his best to convince Mussolini that an even tighter alliance between their two countries would be of benefit to Italy and also might influence the Holy See towards softening its denunciations of Nazism. For this purpose Hitler decided to visit Rome. While no official request was made, the German Embassy did put out delicate unofficial enquiries to learn if His Holiness would be disposed to grant an audience to the Führer.

The Germanic feelers dropped into a dough of silence, and three days before Hitler's visit the Pope and Pacelli, together with their staff, left Rome for the Pope's country residence, Castel Gandolfo, so that their eyes need not look upon "the crooked cross that was not the Cross of Christ."

Pacelli planned a further snub for the Nazi dictator. When Hitler expressed a desire to see the wonders of the Sistine Chapel and the superb collection of art in the Vatican Museum, he was told that it was "closed for repairs".

In September, 1938, came the Czechoslovakian crisis, when Hitler demanded the Sudetenland, and for two fearful weeks Europe teetered on the verge of war. The British Prime Minister, Neville Chamberlain, carried his famous umbrella to Munich and purchased peace, not 'for our time', but for a scant year, by throwing the Czechs to the Nazi wolves.

What Pacelli thought of this surrender is not recorded, but it may be inferred from his comment to the French Ambassador when Hitler marched into the Rhineland in 1935. At that time Pacelli said that it was unfortunate that France had not opposed such a violation of international agreements. Pacelli was not an appeaser.

In January, 1939, poor Chamberlain, with his symbolic furled umbrella, came to Rome. With him came Lord Halifax, who was the archtype of British aristocrat devoting his life to public service. Indeed, Halifax had such an easy manner that he even managed to make his wooden arm and artificial hand an attribute of elegance.

The two men were received in a private audience by Pope Pius XI and had a long conference with Pacelli. The cardinal could not share Chamberlain's buoyant hopes of peace, but regarded the Munich agreement as worthless. It was evident that Halifax found the mendicant's rôle distasteful.

February 11, 1939, was the tenth anniversary of the signing of the Lateran Pact and coincided with the ageing Pope's sixtieth year as a priest. A celebration was planned; and Pius and Pacelli began drafting an address which they hoped might yet stem mankind's downward drift. Sick as he was, the Pope refused to conserve his energy. Pacelli, worried by the amount of work the Pontiff was putting in on the speech, begged him to take more rest. To this Pius flashed the reply, "The Church is better off with a dead Pope than with a Pope who cannot work."

The inevitable happened. On the evening of February 9, the Holy Father suffered another heart attack. Doctors were called, who pronounced it slight, and, when Pius was made comfortable for the night, Pacelli allowed himself to be persuaded to go to bed.

But he could not sleep. At five o'clock in the morning of February 10, Pacelli was already dressed and working in his room when he heard confused murmurs outside his door, and a gentle knock. Not even pausing to ask a question, since he knew in his heart the answer, he went swiftly down the marble corridors to the Pope's apartment.

He was only just in time to kneel beside the bed of the man who had offered his life for the peace of the world. With his hand clasped in that of his friend and adviser, Achille Ratti died.

Wearily Pacelli rose from his knees, and gently folded the dead Pope's arms across his breast. Then he stooped down and lightly kissed his friend's serene forehead.

*

CHAPTER THIRTEEN

THE TRIPLE CROWN

THE Pope is officially Supreme Pontiff from the moment of his election, but his coronation has always been looked upon as the symbolic expression of his assumption of that high office. Eugenio Pacelli was elected on March 2, 1939. He named March 12 as the day of his coronation. In order that the spiritual impact of the ceremony should be as effective as possible, he decided that the coronation should be held in full view of the people of Rome.

This would be the first time since before the fall of Rome in 1870 that a Pope had been crowned in public, and the news raced like a flash fire through the city, filling every home with eagerness. The excitement was especially intense in his own quarter, the Monte Giordano, where everyone joyfully anticipated seeing one of their own people assume the triple crown.

Though there are nearly four hundred churches in Rome, St. Peter's was the traditional place for the ceremony, since its vast spaces and magnificence lent themselves to the importance of the occasion. The Mass would be said inside the basilica, but the crowning would take place on the balcony in full view of the great square. The new Pope ordered that

the floor of the balcony be raised to the height of the para-
pet, making a stage that everyone could see.

The *San Pietrini* worked furiously preparing the interior
of the church. Pacelli's innate good taste curbed the exuber-
ance of those who were in immediate charge, and the scheme
of decoration was kept simple, the lighting subdued and
restrained. Red, white and yellow were the colours used—
red, the colour of the martyrs and the city of Rome; yellow
and white, the papal colours. The myriad facets of the huge
chandeliers of brilliant cut glass diffused the light and
deepened the red of the velvet and brocade draperies suspended from the many pillars. Waves of yellow light sifted
down from the dome, whose golden mosaics reflected the
lamps hidden in the friezes and brought out in sharp relief
the black lettering: "Thou art Peter, and upon this rock I
will build my Church."

Directly under the dome stands the baldachin, the canopy.
It is an enormous structure ninety-five feet high made
entirely of bronze thought to have been taken from the roof
of the Pantheon by Pope Urban VIII. The canopy is heavily
ornamented with gilt and is supported by four twisted
columns. Under it is the High Altar, which stands above
the original small oratory built above the grave of St. Peter
by Anacletus in the year 90 A.D. Only the Pope or a specially
authorised cardinal may celebrate Mass at the High Altar.

At the back of the basilica, under a glory of stained glass,
stands the Chair of St. Peter. It is of wood inset with ivory,
and is said to have been used by the Apostle himself.
Enclosing it, is another chair of gilt bronze supported by
the colossal figures of four Fathers of the Church. For the
coronation, a splendid piece of white silk brocade, bestrewn

with flowers worked in golden thread, was draped beneath
the chair of St. Peter, and in front of this was placed the
high papal throne, simple and white.

Eugenio Pacelli, now sixty-three years old, was up very
early the day of the ceremony. He spent a long hour in
silent prayer and meditation, strengthening himself for the
ordeal. At about 7.15 he started for the Sacristy accompanied
by the papal chamberlains and attendant monsignori. There
they helped him to vest for the processional entry into the
cathedral.

The robing took more than an hour, as the many ceremonial garments were one by one placed upon him. The
Pope's tall, ascetic figure seemed to bow under the enormous
weight of his vestments, and when he moved there were
deep imprints of his narrow feet in the thick carpet on which
he stood. But Pius's face was unmoved, except for a moment
when he raised his luminous black eyes to the cross above
the cupboards, and asked help from One who also bore a
heavy burden.

The procession had already formed near the courtyard of
St. Damaso, and the Pontiff now took his place at its end.
Down the broad marble steps of the Scala Regia, the Royal
Stairs, it wound into the columned portico of St. Peter's. It
halted before the Holy Door, which is opened but once every
quarter century in the Holy Year. Pius slowly walked towards the door, and seated himself on a small throne that
had been placed in front of it. The canons of St. Peter's,
forming a double file, came forward and offered their
homage to Pius XII.

The Pope accepted it and thanked them for their welcome

to the Church. Already the taut skin of his face showed the emotional and physical strain under which he laboured, but his voice was strong and clear.

Now the *sedia gestatoria,* the huge white and gilt sedan chair of ceremony, was brought forward. The Pope stepped into it, and was raised to the shoulders of the stalwart guards who followed the procession into the Church.

By six o'clock that morning, St. Peter's had been filled by a congregation of more than 70,000 people. In the tribune reserved for them sat the members of the diplomatic corps in full ceremonial dress of gold-laced uniforms. Their wives were all in black, with mantillas of exquisite lace covering their heads. In another tribune sat the Knights of Malta wearing black capes illumined by a white cross, and near them the Knights of the Holy Sepulchre in cloaks of white emblazoned with a scarlet cross. The blue and saffron of the Swiss Guards, standing stiffly to attention in various parts of the cathedral, brought warm undertones of colour, and the polished steel of their breast-plates were pin-pointed with sparks of light. The enormously long centre aisle down which the Pope would come was lined all the way by the Palatine Guard, resplendent in their colourful costumes of red and blue.

All the bells of Rome had been pealing thunderous joy since early morning. At 8.45 they all stopped at once, and the sudden silence seemed a physical thing. Then the soft vibrancy of music was felt rather than heard as the procession entered the basilica. At its head walked the habited superiors of the religious orders. They were followed by the papal valets in red-flowered damask. Then came the monsignori in their red cassocks, befurred with white, the glow-ing purple of the bishops, the vibrant scarlet of the cardinals. The vested prelates carried white silk cushions on which rested their mitres. On one cushion, larger than the rest, gleamed the triple crown. Last came the Pope, himself, carried high above all heads between the gently stirring plumes of white ostrich feather fans; a frail figure in the enshrouding folds of his vestments of white, gold-laced silk. His fine features were rigid, his eyes enraptured, seeming lost in the immensity of the Almighty.

But from the high, gently swaying *sedia gestatoria,* Eugenio Pacelli could see in the shadowy vastness of the Church an infinity of faces turned towards him, and occasionally his features relaxed and his eyes smiled as he raised his hand to impart the papal blessing to his right and to his left.

At the altar of St. Gregory, the ceremonial chair was gently lowered to the floor, and Pius stepped out. He assumed the vestments of the celebrant of the Mass. But before Pius moved again towards the High Altar, a server, holding a silver salver on which were three balls of flax, moved before him. The server set one of the flaxen balls on fire, and, as it flared fiercely and died, he said in loud tones, *"Sic transit gloria mundi!"*

Three times he performed this rite; and each time Pius gravely acknowledged the reminder of the evanescence of earthly glory.

Around the Pope's shoulders now was placed the pallium, a long strip of white wool into which are woven black crosses, which is the symbol of jurisdiction. As the Mass began with all the solemnity accumulated through nineteen centuries, he took his place on the throne underneath the

Chair of St. Peter. The rite proceeded through its stately course. The Epistle and the Gospel were sung in Latin and Greek. At the Consecration, Pius came forward and elevated the Host to the four corners of the earth. A blare of silver trumpets rang out from high up in the dome, accompanied by a metallic clash as the guards presented arms.

After the last Gospel, His Holiness turned from the Altar and facing the multitude, like a white flame in his jewelled chasuble, imparted his three-fold blessing.

When the Mass was over the Provost presented the Holy Father with a purse in which were twenty-five golden coins —the Mass stipend. In accepting it Pius knew that he was acknowledging his office as a priest. He gravely thanked the Provost, and passed the heavy purse to his train-bearer.

The procession now re-formed and moved back up the aisle. In its intense emotion the congregation could no longer be restrained and surging forward threatened to break through the cordon of Palatine Guards. They wanted to get near to the Holy Father, to hear his voice again. They were like children running to the head of the family, and, as that lonely white figure was carried slowly down the aisle, it seemed to them that the love of Pius for his people flowed over and embraced them.

Emotion became too exalted for decorous silence. The murmuring undertones grew and swelled and burst out in an irrepressible ovation. All the languages of earth were mingled in one great voice that echoed and re-echoed from chapel to chancel roof and thundered through the dome, while the great sparkling chandeliers swayed and tinkled to the sound and the red draperies stirred and rustled.

As his love had gone out to them, the strength of his people seemed to enter Pius's body. The bent shoulders straightened under the heavy robes, his head was high, and his face was radiant with the light of happiness.

The crowd waiting in St. Peter's Square was so great, no man could guess its numbers. The people had climbed on parapets and window-ledges and perched precariously on top of the chimneys. Into that vast assemblage, the con-gregation, seventy thousand strong, issuing from St. Peter's, slowly forced its way. This took a long time, and it was after midday when the papal standard bearer appeared on the balcony facing the Square and set the banner of the Church beside the throne on the platform. He retired, and soon a cascade of mitre-crested cardinals and bishops in scarlet and purple poured through the large windows, and ranged themselves to the right and left of the standard. A little moment passed, and the Pope in gleaming white appeared at the entrance, hesitated for an instant in the face of the heaven-splitting crash of cheers, and then walked for-ward to seat himself on the throne.

The coronation itself was surprisingly brief. A cardinal-deacon stepped towards the throne, and removed the mitre from the Holy Father's head. As he backed away, the senior cardinal-deacon came forward, holding the triple crown in his outstretched hands. There was a flurry of scarlet silk as he made his obeisance. Holding the tiara over the Pontiff, he said in slow clear tones, "Receive the tiara adorned with three crowns, and know that you are the Father of princes and kings, the Pastor of the Universe and the Vicar on earth of Our Lord Jesus Christ, to whom belongs honour and glory, now and forever, world without end."

Then he slowly lowered the crown on to the dark head before him.

That was all, but, as the weight of the great tiara pressed down on Pius's brow, the full import of the ancient formula exalted his mind. He was Ruler, Father, Vicar, and he was no longer afraid.

Still crowned with the tiara, Pius raised himself and, descending the podium, walked to the balustrade. Slight though he was, the majesty of the Church seemed to enlarge him, as he stretched out his arms to all that throng, and all the world. His voice rang clear and sonorous as he said, "May the blessing of Almighty God, Father, Son and Holy Ghost descend upon you, and remain with you forever!"

*

CHAPTER FOURTEEN

"THE FORCES OF

GODLESSNESS"

No one in the whole troubled world of 1939 was more aware of the terrible danger of war than Pope Pius XII. He did not delay an instant in starting his campaign for peace. Even before his coronation, on the day after his election, he was early at work, receiving members of the Diplomatic Corps and writing an address to the College of Cardinals that was broadcast to the world.

At mid-morning he descended to the Sistine Chapel, the scene of his election the previous day. Deep in concentration he passed through an eager and excited throng waiting to catch a glimpse of him in the mighty Hall of Dukes, and entered the Chapel. It was still arranged as on the day of his election. On each side of him were the stalls with their canopies now lowered. Each was occupied by a cardinal. The Pope's tall and lonely figure, all in white, moved slowly between the banks of red billowing silk until he reached the seat he had occupied yesterday, still covered with its purple canopy, for it had become the throne.

Pius seated himself on it, and the cardinals one by one

approached him to offer their homage. Softly their lips touched his slim white hand, then bending low they kissed his gold-embroidered, white slipper.

When the act of obeisance was over, Pius spoke to the College of Cardinals and over microphones to the world. *'Dum Gravissimum'* he called his address and at the close of it he said: "We wish to add an invitation to, and an augury of peace. We speak of the peace for which Our predecessor offered his life, the peace which joins nations and peoples in brotherly love. . . . We pray to God for all who are placed in authority over states upon whom falls the burden of leading their peoples in the way of peace."

During the ten days between his election and his coronation, Pius worked nearly twenty-one hours a day, averaging three hours sleep a night. There were so many messages to answer; so many visitors to greet. Among those who came to offer congratulations and good wishes was Eamon de Valera, first president of the Irish Republic, who stayed with the Pope for more than an hour. American Ambassador to London Joseph P. Kennedy and his large family were received in private audience.

Protestants as well as Catholics sent messages of good will. President Roosevelt telegraphed recalling their meeting at Hyde Park. George VI of England sent the Duke of Norfolk, Premier Duke of England, to represent him at the coronation. For the first time in history the Patriarch of Constantinople announced his intention of representing the Greek Orthodox Church at the ceremony in St. Peter's.

All these things offset a little of the danger of the totalitarian challenge to Christianity.

The day before his coronation, Pius appointed Cardinal

Maglione as his Secretary of State to help him with the "Government of the Bark of Peter to steer it amidst so many waves and tempests toward the port of peace." The cardinal had served the Holy See for many years as Nuncio in Paris, and before that he had been responsible for concluding the concordat with Switzerland in 1920. When Cardinal Maglione died in 1944, he was not replaced. Pius became his own Secretary of State.

When Maglione was promoted, Monsignor Domenico Tardini was made head of the Vatican Foreign Office. The more suave members of the Papal Court considered Tardini a rather rough diamond. He is a little fighting cock of a man, pug-nosed and peppery. His manner seems abrupt to the point of rudeness, but he is the tough-tender kind. His only 'recreation' is supervising a small home for orphan boys called the Villa Nazareth, located about two miles from Rome. There Tardini spends most of his free time, and virtually all of his money.

Monsignor Giovanni Battista Montini, who became Pius's Secretary of Ordinary Ecclesiastical Affairs, is Tardini's opposite in appearance and character. A tall thin man with a swarthy complexion and intense dark eyes, he is a tremendous worker. Because of his interest in social problems he became, in effect, the Holy See's labour relations expert and has done more than any other prelate to win Italian labour away from the false friendship of communism.

In January, 1939, when Cardinal Pacelli had told the Prime Minister, Neville Chamberlain, that Hitler's signature of the Munich Pact was worthless, even he did not expect to be proved right so soon. On March 15, three days after Pius XII was crowned, Hitler invaded Czechoslovakia and annexed it to the Reich. The democratic powers just stood by and watched. Encouraged by this, on Good Friday, April 7, Mussolini reached out his armoured paw and scooped in little Albania.

In these barefaced aggressions, Pius saw his worst fears for the future foreshadowed. But he dared not give up hope. In his sermon on Easter Sunday, April 9, the Holy Father sternly asked, "How can there be a real and solid peace when even men of the same nationality are torn apart by intrigues in the interest of political parties . . . when solemnly sanctioned treaties are violated?"

There was criticism in the democratic countries because the Pope had not come right out and named the aggressors. But Pius knew that to do so would be to lose all influence with them, and he was determined to keep the Vatican above national disputes. So he firmly kept back the words he was raging to say . . . because he had not given up hope.

Indeed, both Mussolini and Hitler were wooing the Holy See at this time in the hope that because of their anti-communist stand, the Pope would help soften world opinion about them. That hope was fruitless, but the diplomatic Pope played upon it so that he might check the aggressors, at least for a while. Mussolini's son-in-law, the Foreign Minister, Count Galleazzo Ciano, had a long talk with Pius, and reported to his master, "I have seen the new Pope, and I think we will get along quite well together."

The German Ambassador to the Holy See, Diego von Bergen, was also received in private audience. He lectured the Pope on "The new rôle he would have to play in the Europe of the young nations," and told him that, "There are some things that no longer have a reason for existing," and that he "hoped the evolution would be peaceful."

Puis was polite to him, and kept on trying in his own way.

Not that he was able to do much. Hitler tore up his naval treaty with England, and then turned loose a barrage of propaganda against Poland. Like every informed European, Pius knew that it was Warsaw's turn next.

Actually, the widespread hierarchy of the Church kept Pius very well informed indeed. He knew far ahead of time that Germany and Russia were about to sign the non-aggression, mutual-aid pact which enabled Hitler to fight a one-front war against France and England. He also knew, almost to a day, the timing of Hitler's proposed attack on Poland.

In a desperate attempt to stem the rush towards war, Pius sent Archbishop Cesare Orsenigo, the Papal Nuncio in Berlin, to see Hitler at Berchtesgaden with a proposal that a conference be held between the major powers of Europe in one last try for a peaceful settlement. Hitler's answer was obviously, "No!"

To the same proposition the democratic powers were less adamant, but rather coy. England wanted more elucidation. France doubted that the time was ripe. The delay was fatal.

Pius did not stop, but redoubled his efforts. He was handicapped by the fact that he could offer no solutions on territorial questions, but the Vatican was used as a clearing house where the problems could be sorted out and reduced to a minimum.

The long Roman spring had turned to hot summer when, in the middle of May, Pius was enthroned as Bishop of

Rome. Again he made history when he decided to revive
the custom that had lapsed for over a century. He commanded that the enthroning take place, not in the Vatican
or St. Peter's, but in the Basilica of St. John Lateran, which
is the titular Church of the Bishop of Rome.

It was a lovely summer morning when Pius left the Vatican
and drove in an open car up the Via della Conciliazione over
the Ponte Vittorio spanning the winding Tiber, and along
the Corso Vittorio Emmanuele, where merchants and clerks
from hundreds of small shops cheered wildly, and fell on
their knees to receive the papal blessing.

Pius passed by his own beloved Chiesa Nuova, where he
first assisted at the Mass. From the tunnel-like streets of his
native quarter poured children laden with flowers which
they scattered in his path like scented snow. From windows
and balconies draped with carpets and tapestries, people who
had called the Pope "neighbour" shouted a roar of welcome.

The papal procession moved on past the melancholy ruins
of the Forum, circled the crumbling Colosseum and turned
into the square confronting the Lateran. It was guarded by
crack troops of the Italian Army and the Pope's own Palatine
Guards in cuirasses and plumed helmets.

As his car stopped, Pius sat for a moment looking at the
old stone façade of "the mother and head of all churches in
the city and the world," which for eight hundred years from
the sixth to the fourteenth century was the principal seat of
the Papacy. He glanced upwards for a moment at the long
line of statues silhouetted against the bronze-blue of the sky.
Then he descended from the car and entered the basilica
through the massive bronze doors that once had been the
entrance to the Roman Senate.

After the Mass was said, Pius, crowned with the mitre, symbol of his bishopric, took his place on the ancient episcopal throne. The canons of the basilica—the oldest chapter of canons in existence, which was founded by Pope Leo I in 440 A.D.—acknowledged him as their head. Gravely he replied, taking formal possession of his church.

When this ceremony was over, heralds in medieval pageantry appeared on the loggia above the main entrance. They carried silver trumpets, with emblazoned banners, on which they sounded a blast. The Holy Father, in gleaming white, contrasting with the brilliant colours of the heraldic banners, walked to the edge of the balcony and gave his benediction to his people.

Then he returned to the Vatican and the final phase of his fight for peace.

In the following months there was a great coming and going of diplomats in the Vatican; prelates and nuncios were sent on new missions. The Secretaries of the nunciatures in Paris, Madrid, Belgrade, Bucharest and London and the Apostolic Delegate to the United States were summoned to Rome to advise the Pope. Pius took personal charge of all these secret negotiations, with only Cardinal Maglione in his confidence. Despite his efforts the situation daily got worse, as fear gathered like clouds in the hearts of men.

On August 19, the anniversary of the death of Pius X, the Holy Father spoke to a great number of pilgrims assembled at Castel Gandolfo. Again his words were carried by radio to the world as he said: "We have not yet abandoned hope that the governments will realise their responsibilities to preserve their peoples from so great a disaster, the terrible responsibility of an appeal to force."

On August 24, he tried again in another broadcast in which he cried, "May all who carry the responsibility of the nations listen to the voice of Christ beyond Our voice. Thus I speak to you leaders of peoples, politicians, men of arms, writers and broadcasters and as many others as have authority over the thoughts and actions of their brothers and responsibility for their faith. We who are armed with nothing but the sword of truth, We speak to you in the name of God. . . . We make to the rulers and peoples our most heartfelt appeal —to the rulers that they lay aside the threat to arms, and try to resolve the present arguments by the only right method, by considered agreements—And to the peoples We appeal that they may encourage the peaceful attempts of their governments.

"Justice is advanced with reason, not with arms. Conquests and empires not founded on justice do not receive the blessing of God.

"The danger is tremendous, but there is still time. Nothing is lost by peace; all is lost by war !"

The Pope's last desperate measure was taken on August 31, when he called the ambassadors of Germany, Poland, Italy, France and England to the Vatican to receive notes beseeching "in the Name of God" that Germany and Poland do everything possible to avoid an incident, and asking the other powers to support this plea. Pius also proposed that these five powers meet with the European neutrals and also the United States and, if they desired, the Vatican.

England, France and, surprisingly, Mussolini, gave instant support to this request. A faint ray of hope appeared when

Hitler told Nuncio Orsenigo that he would receive a Polish Envoy.

That night Pius sat long at his desk, pondering, writing and hoping. He finally went to bed. It seemed he had been asleep for but a moment when the telephone broke the silence with shrill alarm. As Pius answered it, Cardinal Maglione's shaken voice told him that Nuncio Orsenigo had reported that Nazi troops were crossing the Polish border.

Pius sat rigid for a long time, too stunned to think. Then he fled to his little chapel and, weeping like a child, flung himself to his knees and poured out his grief to his Father.

Pius learned how horrible modern war could be when August Cardinal Hlond, the Primate of Poland, who fled the Nazi onslaught at the last moment as bombed-out Warsaw fell, came to report at Castel Gandolfo on September 21. So moved was Pius that in his encyclical of October, 1939, he wrote: "The pen might well fall from Our hand when we think of the countless disasters that are happening to those who until now had only happiness in their private lives.

"The blood of countless human beings, including non-combatants, raises a dirge over Our dear Poland . . . (which) has a right to the brotherly sympathy of the whole world while it awaits, relying on the powerful intercessions of Mary Help of Christians, the hour of resurrection in harmony with the principles of justice and true peace." Thus he threw the whole authority of the Church in the face of the German and Russian partition of Poland.

He went further, for he continued to recognise the Polish Government in Exile as a free and independent state, and sent Monsignor Pacini as Chargé d'Affaires to them.

Nor did Pius mince words when a little later Russia attacked Finland. He referred to this in delightfully undiplomatic terms as "actions which cry to heaven for vengeance."

One of Pius's first acts on returning to the Vatican in October was to fling another challenge in the teeth of the racists. He raised to the Episcopate twelve missionary bishops, who, as he said, were, "representatives of the nations from which they come." Among them were a Negro, a Chinese, an Indian and a priest from Madagascar. Thus he was putting into effect the universality of the Church.

The consecration took place in St. Peter's. The slow file of bishops-to-be approached the Throne of St. Peter, and laid their traditional gifts of a pair of lighted torches, two tiny gilded casks of wine and two loaves of bread at the Pontiff's feet. As Pius accepted the gifts in the name of the Infant to whom the Magi had brought their offerings two thousand years ago, he looked at the white, brown, yellow and black faces before him and there came into his mind the words of Christ, "Teach you all nations."

The Pope's immediate effort was to keep Italy out of the war, and to prevent the spread of battle areas. President Franklin D. Roosevelt of the United States was working along the same lines. He wanted very much to establish direct contact beween Pius and himself. There had been no diplomatic relations between the Holy See and the United States since 1868; and because of American prejudices it did not seem expedient to establish them formally now. To get around this difficulty, the President suggested to Monsignor Amleto Cicognani, the Apostolic Delegate in Washington, that he send a personal envoy to Pius. The Pope liked the idea, and Roosevelt appointed the Pope's former friend in New York, Myron Taylor.

It was an excellent choice. Taylor was not a Catholic, but he was well known in Italy, where he frequently lived at his villa in Florence. The Pope had conceived a strong liking for both Mr. and Mrs. Taylor, and knew of the former's work as President of the Committee to Care for Political Refugees. Taylor accepted the appointment on December 22, 1939. That same day Roosevelt wrote a personal letter to Pius, calling him "My old and very good friend" and sending him "a message of greeting and faith," and urging co-operation in their joint efforts for peace.

When Myron Taylor reached Rome, Pius received him, not in the formal Hall of Thrones, but in the Hall of the Little Throne, tactfully to emphasise his unofficial standing. In a series of conferences they discussed joint American and Papal moves towards peace, or at least to limit the fighting and alleviate the misery it caused.

Even before Taylor reached Rome the Pope proposed a five-point plan for peace in an allocution to the cardinals on Christmas Eve 1939. The five points in substance were:

1. The acknowledgment of the right of all nations great and small to security and independence; "The will of one nation to live must never mean the sentence of death passed on another."
2. The necessity that nations free themselves of the "slavery" of the armament race.
3. The reinvigoration or creation of "international institutions."
4. The establishment of proper regard for the rights of racial minorities.

5. The recognition that the nations should work, not against, but with the divine law.

These five points later were adapted by Roosevelt and Winston Churchill as the basis of their inspiring Atlantic Charter. For the moment the Pope's proposals met with polite approbation from the world. So on the first Christmas of the war he brought a faint ray of daylight to the embattled peoples. The collaboration of the United States and the Holy See; Mussolini's indecision about entering the war and Hitler's peace feelers indicated that the door to peace might be ajar. Pius was too practical a diplomat to pin much faith on these things, but he at least could hope. And pray.

In March, 1940, Hitler sent Foreign Minister Joachim von Ribbentrop to bring Mussolini up to date on his war plans. The Nazi champagne salesman asked for a private audience with the Pope. Pius, who would see anybody in the interests of peace, received him.

On the day after his arrival in Rome, von Ribbentrop drove to see the Pope in a curious motorcade. From the mud-guards of his car flew the German Swastika and the Papal colours, and the same flags fluttered on the bonnets of the Italian police cars. But leading the procession and bringing up the rear were Vatican Cadillacs flying no flags at all. There were no cheers as the Nazi drove through the capital of his ally—only the stony silence of disapproval.

Von Ribbentrop in his gold-leafed, Swastika-embellished uniform swaggered into the Pope's office accompanied by the Ambassador, Diego von Bergen. After a perfunctory reverence to the Vicar of Christ, the Nazi proceeded to deliver a lecture on *Weltpolitik* to Pius, in which he described the might of the Hitler Reich and pointed out the folly of the Pope's alignment with the democracies.

Pius listened to the guttural bombast with never a change of expression. When the Nazi had done, he opened a big ledger on his desk, and began to read a documented account of Nazi atrocities in Poland. It was complete with names, dates, places, details and witnesses. As he turned the leaves of the great tome and read on in a level voice, the slight figure in white sitting at his desk seemed to take on some quality of the Recording Angel on Judgment Day.

Von Ribbentrop did not wait for him to finish. Saluting stiffly, he stalked red-faced from the room, trailed by his ambassador. It was all too much for poor von Bergen, who suffered a complete collapse a short time later.

Though Pius now had no hope of peace from Germany, he renewed his efforts to influence Mussolini, bringing all sorts of pressure to bear. Prior to this, in December, 1939, the King and Queen of Italy had paid a formal visit to the Vatican with full ceremony—a gesture intended to show the world in general and Italy in particular that they, at least, were on the side of the angels.

Much later, on December 14, 1941, Victor Emmanuel further defied the Duce and showed his regard for Pius by creating the Pope's three nephews, Carlo, Marcantonio and Giulio Pacelli, hereditary princes of the Kingdom of Italy.

Immediately after Christmas, Pius had himself driven to the vast Palace of the Quirinal to return the royal call. But Mussolini had no more regard for his king than for the wishes of the Italian people.

In March, 1940, Hitler met Mussolini at the Brenner Pass. When Mussolini got back to Rome, the Papal Nuncio to Italy reported to Pius that the infatuated Duce would follow Hitler's lead.

In April, 1940, the period of military inactivity known in America as "The Phony War," ended with a crash as Hitler's legions took Denmark and invaded Norway. On April 24, Pius again wrote to Mussolini begging him to remain neutral, and during the next month President Roosevelt sent three messages to the Italian dictator through the American Ambassador, William Phillips, urging and warning him to keep out of the war.

The hardest blow soon fell. On May 10, 1940, Hitler launched his armoured might against the small neutral nations of Holland and Belgium. The centre of Rotterdam was devastated in twenty frightful minutes of dive bombing as a warning to those who dared to oppose German conquest. The triumphant Panzers swept on to crush the French and British armies in the Low Countries, and enveloped the Maginot Line.

Until now Pius had tried desperately to keep the Church above the battle, but this was too much. He sent moving telegrams of condolence to the governments of Luxemburg and Belgium, promising to pray for them. To Protestant Queen Wilhelmina of Holland he wrote: "We beg God, the Supreme Ruler of mankind, that, as quickly as possible, He may restore justice and liberty." At the same time the *Osservatore Romano* bluntly stated that the Nazi decision to invade and annex peaceful neutrals could not be justified either morally or politically.

Mussolini was furious. He had called the Papacy "a disease wasting away the life of Italy," and vowed that he would "rid himself of this turbulent priest." Now he took violent measures. The delivery boys collected at the Vatican that morning as usual to pick up the *Osservatore Romano* for delivery to all parts of the city. As they came out of the Pope's palace with their bundles of papers, they were attacked by Fascist "liquidation squads," armed with bicycle chains, barbed wire, razors and all sorts of lethal weapons. The boys dropped their papers and fled screaming, pursued by the savage Blackshirts, who beat them unmercifully.

Other gangs gathered up the papers which were publicly burned by the Fascist government. At the same time orders went out to confiscate all copies sent through the mails.

The Foreign Minister, Count Ciano, still had some sense left. He realised that such an attack in the shadow of the Vatican would produce a world-wide reaction far more deleterious to Fascism than a newspaper editorial. He immediately instructed the Italian Ambassador to the Holy See, Dino Alfieri, to apologise, and try to arrange an agreement whereby the Holy See would tone down its attitude towards the Axis powers.

No one who had been received in the friendly informality of a peace-time private audience would have recognised Pius that day. He was as stern as the Angel of Death, and as dedicated as St. Peter before his crucifixion. He stated that he would always proclaim the right of any nation to defend itself against unprovoked aggression. Nor would he deny, by silence, the expression of his views. "Your government has the power to put Us in a concentration camp if it wishes," he told Alfieri. "But We will do nothing against Our conscience."

Late in May the full strength of the Nazi armies burst upon

the weakened defences of France, and rolled over them like a flood of steel and fire. On June 10, they were at the gates of Paris. Now Mussolini felt it was time for him to take his jackal's share of the loot. He declared war on France, and sent his armies crawling over the Alpine passes.

In an impassioned speech that day, President Roosevelt said, "The hand that held a dagger has struck it into the back of his neighbour."

The same dagger pierced the very heart of Pius XII.

*

CHAPTER FIFTEEN

THE OPEN CITY

Now that Italy had become a belligerent the Vatican State was isolated in the midst of the raging torrent of war. Pius was grimly determined to preserve its neutral status. He ordered air-raid shelters to be built and special steel vaults constructed in which to preserve the most valuable manuscripts and art treasures of the Vatican. A rigid black-out was enforced, and in the blank façade of the palace the Pope's beacon light no longer burned.

Since Vatican City was an independent state, Pius was able to bring the ambassadors and representatives of the belligerents who were accredited to the Holy See within its walls. They and their families were housed in its many splendid rooms, where they lived as though in a besieged city. It was impossible for them to go out, nor were they allowed to receive visitors.

Later, when the Nazis took over Rome, this right of sanctuary was extended to all manner of people. Just before the Allies liberated Rome some thousands of refugees, including hundreds of Jews, were camped in the great palace, around which the majesty of the Vicar of Christ had drawn what Bulwer-Lytton's Cardinal Richelieu called, "The awful circle of our Holy Church."

Those who were cared for directly by the Vatican were only a small percentage of the distressed people succoured by the efforts of Pius XII. Early in the war the Pope had formed the Pontifical Relief Committee to give immediate assistance to the unfortunate war victims of all nations in the form of such concrete things as medicines, food, goods and cash. Through this committee the Vatican became a great clearing house where donations from all the world were received and transmitted through relief centres and field missions, around and even inside the devastated countries, and to the prisoners of war in their wretched prison camps. Pius enlisted the whole great organisation of the Catholic Church and its auxiliaries in this Christian war against man-made misery. After Italy entered the war, much of this work was carried on from neutral Portugal under the direction of Federico's son, Marquis Carlo Pacelli.

Pius also established a system of Vatican agents throughout Europe. But his 'spies' sought no military information, but only news of hundreds of thousands of men and women lost to their families, who had sought his aid in finding their loved ones.

After Italy entered the war there intervened a long uncertain period, during which the dictators controlled all Europe, from the outskirts of Moscow to the Pyrenees, save only the little, beleaguered British island and neutral Switzerland. But Pius continued to work for a peace of which even he had little hope.

Nor did he in any way compromise with his conscience. When Hitler attacked Russia in June, 1941, proclaiming his holy war against Communism, both dictators looked hopefully at the Vatican for moral support. Pius gave them no comfort whatever, but continued to inveigh against all forms of totalitarianism. At the same time, though Russia was now an ally of the democracies, the Pope did not fool himself as to the ultimate danger of Communism. He just reckoned that the Axis type of dictatorship was temporarily more dangerous to Christianity.

Oddly enough, the greatest period of stress and also of personal danger to the Holy Father came just when the peril of a Nazi-Fascist victory began to lessen. When the United States entered the war after the Japanese attack on Pearl Harbor, her enormous military potential swung the balance of power to the side of the democracies. At first the only difference this made was further to embitter and harden the attitude of the Nazi Government. But when in November, 1942, American and British forces invaded North Africa, and began their encirclement of the German-Italian armies which had so nearly taken Egypt and the British life line of the Suez Canal, both the Italian people and the Pope feared that Rome itself might become a battleground.

To Pius this was the last, worst threat. He cared nothing about his personal safety; but he cared tremendously that Rome, with all its historical and artistic treasures, the heart of Western civilisation and the very cradle of the Church, should not suffer a holocaust. He began to negotiate with all the belligerent powers to have Rome declared an 'open city'.

This objective was confused by the fact that Rome was, in fact, a legitimate military target. Italian Army, Air Force and Navy commands were stationed in the city, and there were German forces there as well. Munition dumps and military airports ringed the city. Even more important was the fact that Rome was a central point of the spider's web of Italian railroads. Through its great marshalling yards passed all the trains bearing troops and military supplies to the southern half of the Italian peninsula and the heavily defended island of Sicily.

Despite this, Pius had long hoped that the Allies would agree to some arrangement that would spare the city, and they had secretly given him reason for optimism. On December 6, 1942, the Pope queried the Italian Ambassador to the Holy See about the possibility of removing the Italian and German commands from Rome. To his amazement and relief Mussolini sent word that he would not only do so, but would himself go elsewhere. At which point the British Foreign Minister, Anthony Eden, indicated that this was not enough. The King and the whole government would have to go as well, and Swiss inspection teams must be allowed to keep watch on the observance of these conditions. Mussolini was wild with rage. At the same time the Pope's secret information was that the United States opposed any bombing of Rome. For these reasons the deal fell through.

Ever since 1940, there had been a strong feeling that the Pope should leave Rome and take refuge in some neutral country, preferably in the Western hemisphere. In February, 1943, Archbishop Francis J. Spellman, a very unofficial emissary of President Roosevelt, discussed it with him. But Pius was adamant against this. He had ordered the Catholic clergy throughout the world to stick to their posts. Should the Bishop of Rome desert his?

Anxiety lessened as the Allied victory in North Africa was won, and still no hostile planes appeared in the Roman sky. On July 10, 1943, British and American troops landed in Sicily and began the systematic liberation of the island. The war had taken a giant stride nearer.

On the morning of July 19, Pius, following his regular routine, received some foreign diplomats in private audience. They were sitting around his great desk chatting informally when, at about eleven o'clock, the howl of air-raid sirens sounded. His Holiness paid no attention—there had been so many drills—but continued the conversation.

A few minutes later the sharp crack of anti-aircraft guns made them all jump. The sound was followed by an ominous earth-shaking boom.

Pius leaped to his feet, and in two quick strides was at the tall windows. He jerked the curtains loose and stood looking over the city. To the east the pale blue sky was dotted by black balls of smoke from the anti-aircraft and, as he stood there, the windows rattled to the blast of more heavy explosions. A thick column of smoke and dust spiralled slowly upward. Other columns followed, spreading and joining until they formed a huge cloud of disaster.

Pius could see that the target was the great railroad terminal and yards. He knew the district well, knew that around the embankment and the yards clustered the ramshackle tenement dwellings of the poor. The diplomats saw his thin shoulders quivering, as he took off his spectacles to wipe away the tears that blurred his sight. Silently they went away, leaving the Pope alone.

For almost two hours the Holy Father stood at the window watching the black cloud thicken and spread across the summer sky; feeling each bomb blast strike his heart. His lips never ceased moving in prayer. Finally he could stand it no longer. He moved decisively to his desk, and picking up the telephone called Monsignor Montini.

"How much cash is there in the Vatican Bank?" he demanded.

"About two million lire, Holiness."

The Pope spoke as crisply as a banker planning a coup. "Draw it out immediately, and take the first car you find in St. Damaso Courtyard. We will join you."

The Holy Father hurried downstairs and met Montini just as he was crossing the courtyard towards a small car parked in the shade. They jumped in quickly and were off through the streets of Rome, on which bombs were still falling, unheralded and unescorted. The car turned down the empty Via della Conciliazione moving rather slowly. "Faster!" Pius ordered. "Go as fast as you can."

With that they fairly flew across the winding, peaceful Tiber, and up the Corso Vittorio Emmanuele. In three minutes they were racing through the Piazza Venezia, turning into the Via Nazionale. In the half light under the smoke pall, the empty streets, usually swarming with jostling life, seemed bleak with catastrophe. Flames streaked the thickening smoke ahead. "Faster!" ordered Pius.

The car crossed the plaza in front of the railway station, from which flames and smoke were billowing, and turned right along the blank wall of the embankment. Ahead were barricades manned by police and soldiers.

As his car stopped Pius stepped out followed by Montini,

clutching his bag of money. Soldiers and civilians made a lane for them, and the murmuring flowed ahead. "Il Papa! Il Papa!" Even in that melancholy moment there was a quality of amazed joy in the voices.

From the officials at the barricades, Pius learned that the ancient Church of San Lorenzo had been partly demolished, and that a bomb had fallen near-by in the cemetery of Campo Verano, where the Pacelli family were buried, scattering the remains of his own father and mother. But he had no time now to lament this.

Into the flame-shot smoke the Holy Father made his way. Now he was in the area of destruction. On his right, beyond the embankment, crackling flames consumed long lines of freight cars with an occasional explosion. On his left were the tottering walls and smoking timbers of shattered houses. Gangs of men dug furiously in piles of rubble, while screams and moans directed them. Bodies and parts of bodies were strewn on the roadway, and the wounded were lying everywhere.

Those who could still stand clustered around the Pope, touching his white cassock with their bloody hands. His people clung to Pius weeping with him in common grief. A workman threw his jacket down on the cobblestones, and the Pope and his people knelt to pray.

When Pius rose he ordered Montini to distribute the money to those who seemed most in need. As he was directing this operation, a distraught mother shoved a small body into his arms. The Holy Father stood tenderly holding the dead child, trying to give consolation to a multitude of mourners.

Meanwhile Montini gave away all the money he had

brought. He gave until the sack was quite empty; while Pius gave consolation until his soul seemed as empty as Montini's money bag. Then begrimed, tear-stained and bloodied, the Holy Father drove back to the Vatican.

The next day Pius addressed a sorrowful letter to President Roosevelt, and an angry one to the Vicar-General of Rome, Francesco Cardinal Marchetti-Selvagiani. It was intended for world consumption, and began: "As Bishop of this sacred City we have constantly tried to save our beloved Rome from devastation. . . . But this reasonable hope has, alas, been frustrated."

On July 25, 1943, Mussolini was arrested by order of the King, and taken to the island of Ponza off Anzio. The Italian people had had enough, and more than enough of the ersatz Imperator. Field-Marshal Pietro Badoglio was appointed head of the Government to succeed him and Rome rejoiced—prematurely it turned out.

Pius immediately brought up the question of declaring Rome an open city. Badoglio was willing to do anything possible, but the Allies were wary. They were not ready to take the revolution at face value or trust the new government.

On August 13, Rome was raided again. This time bombs rained on the district of San Giovanni near the Pope's own church, St. John Lateran. Once more Pius hurried to the scene. Heedless of falling masonry, the Holy Father passed from group to sorrowing group, weeping in sympathy with them. Once again his white cassock was red with blood, his shoes cut by broken glass, and his hands gory from ministering to the wounded.

As he passed by one group he saw a little girl lying on a

stretcher, cold and immobile. Kneeling beside her, he touched her and spoke to her. At the sound of his consoling voice the child opened her eyes as though awakening from sleep. Then she rose from her stretcher and walked.

The next day, August 14, the Allies accepted Badoglio's terms and Rome was declared an open city. On September 8, as American and British troops landed at Salerno on the mainland, Marshal Badoglio's Government anonunced the surrender of Italy.

Secret arrangements had been made to parachute the United States 82nd Airborne Division into Rome, to hold it until the Allies arrived, but when the Nazis sensed trouble and reinforced their troops around the capital, the drop was called off.

At the time of the surrender the King, the royal family and Marshal Badoglio fled secretly from Rome. Field-Marshal Enrico Caviglia took over command of the city. He immediately opened negotiations with the German commander, Field-Marshal Albert Kesselring, to induce him to leave Rome alone.

Of course the Nazis had no intention of doing any such thing, but they played cat-and-mouse with Caviglia until they were ready to strike.

Because of secret information that an attack was imminent, Pius ordered the Papal guards to store their plumed helmets and halberds, and armed them with rifles and machine-guns. On September 10, the Pope ordered the entrance to the Vatican at Porta Santa Anna to be sealed, and the great doors of St. Peter's closed—the first time in all history that they had been shut in the daytime. It was done for fear that masses of people, seeking sanctuary, might be killed if the great basilica were shelled, either by accident or design, in the expected battle for Rome. However, the Romans regarded it as the worst of omens. The city waited, shivering in fear and anger.

Romans breathed easier when Caviglia announced that he had signed an agreement with the Nazis that they withdraw to a line north of the city. But even while Romans were repeating the news to each other, the sirens wailed as shells screamed into Rome.

From the Aventine, Gianicolo, and Pincio Hills, Italian artillery answered the German fire. Shells arced and crossed above the ancient Aurelean wall. The terrible German 88 mm. shells fell on the famous streets and squares of Rome, the Trinita, Via del Tritone, and the Corso. Gradually the big German guns silenced the smaller Italian pieces.

Meanwhile fighting was going on outside the walls. As the confused and outnumbered Italian troops gave way, the enemy poured through the old gates of Rome, and the battle moved into the city itself. The streets of the crowded Trastevere quarter were slippery with blood as the disciplined German troops fought mixed bands of Italian soldiers and civilians.

By six o'clock organised resistance ended, and the Nazis, bloody and dusty, but in ruler-straight formations, marched with ringing boots down the principal streets of Rome. By seven they were in complete control of the city. The Romans retired behind their heavy oaken portals, their closed iron shutters, and time-stained walls to pass a lightless night, disturbed by occasional staccato bursts of machine-gun fire as the last defenders were winkled out of their hide-aways.

*

CHAPTER SIXTEEN

THE

SANCTUARY STANDS

Now Vatican City was truly besieged. For, though even the Nazis dared not break the sacred circle of its ancient walls, they held Rome like a conquered city. Everywhere on its broad avenues and narrow cobbled streets, steel-grey men in wash-basin helmets tramped, with Luger pistols swinging in their holsters; while trucks rumbled up and down the avenues, crowded with soldiers who kept rifles and sub-machine-guns focused on the footpaths.

From his window in the Vatican, Pius could see the German sentries pacing just beyond St. Peter's Square. At night he could hear the barbarian tread stamping on the pavements. Distant bursts of automatic fire brought him to his knees before his altar to pray for the parishioners of the Bishop of Rome.

During the first days of occupation, there was a lot of looting. Rome was like a plague-infected city with the iron shutters down on all its little shops, and lonely figures scurrying fearfully down its usually crowded footpaths. Those few who ventured out were often held up at pistol point and robbed of their watches, and any loose change they might have. Soldiers roamed around 'commandeering' every form of transport from fine automobiles to small motor-cycle delivery vans and even women's bicycles.

Meanwhile, the German Ambassador to the Holy See, Baron von Weizsächer, who was secretly anti-Nazi, was working hard to have the neutrality of Vatican City respected. The Pope had first received Weizsächer on July 5, 1943. He knew him to be a true friend of the Holy See and a fellow worker for peace. In the desperate days of September the German Ambassador justified Pius's confidence. It was he who prevailed on the German High Command in Italy to abide by the law of nations, and respect the Holy Father's domain.

Catholic General Stahel of the Luftwaffe, commanding the city under Field-Marshal Kesselring, restored the famous German discipline. Orders went out that looting would bring the death penalty. On that same day, September 13, 1943, Stahel telephoned the Papal Governor of Vatican City that a formal boundary guard would be set up.

At 4 p.m., Nazi paratroopers in full battle regalia appeared in the Square. There was a conference with the commanders of the Swiss and Palatine Guards, who were also armed to the teeth with modern weapons. Then a broad white line was painted across the pavement from one wing of Bernini's colonnade to the other. On one side of it paced stone-faced Nazis; on the other stood the khaki-clad soldiers of the Pope.

On September 19, 1944, Field-Marshal Kesselring telephoned to request an audience with the Pope. Pius received him, as he had so many more gracious visitors in his office. But as the German marshal strode stiffly in, the Holy Father did not rise as was his courteous custom, but remained seated, thin, white and implacable behind his big desk. Kesselring saluted abruptly, and Pius inclined his head, and invited the marshal to be seated. The latter quickly came to the point. He had given orders that the Vatican and all the Papal possessions such as the churches, basilicas, convents, colleges, and even Castel Gandolfo on its hilltop in the country be held inviolate by his troops. In return, he requested His Holiness to let the world know that the German troops were behaving 'correctly'. Evidently the rumours from Rome circulating throughout the world were getting under even the Nazis' thick skins.

Pius agreed to the Field-Marshal's request. It was his first duty to protect his people and Papal property. If this could be done by telling the truth, it was to the advantage of all. So the following day the *Osservatore Romano* announced that Kesselring's troops were respecting Papal territory and Papal buildings.

When the Germans first occupied Rome, the Italians, and Pius himself, expected that the Allies would soon drive them out. However, it rapidly became evident that the British Eighth Army and the Fifth Army of the American General, Mark Clark, did not have the power. As the Allied thrust from Naples bogged down among the mountain ranges that crossed their path in a series of tremendous natural ramparts, Pius realised that the winter would be long and dour.

Meanwhile, Mussolini had been rescued from his allied captors by a German coup and had set up 'The Fascist Republic of Italy' in northern Italy under the protection of German guns. Now these neo-Fascists moved in on Rome under the governorship of Roberto Farinacci. They were far more vicious than the Germans, who were disciplined troops proud of their esprit, while the new Fascists were renegades thirsting for revenge.

Thus began a strange struggle for the soul of a city. On one side were Nazis and Fascists with all the power of their armoured divisions; their ruthless materialism; and the propaganda machinery of the muzzled press, and every radio station in the city save one, that which Pacelli had fore-sightedly built in Vatican City a decade ago. On the other side was a single white-clad figure surrounded only by his prelates, and a few soldiers who, until a short time before, had worn the fancy dress which Michelangelo had designed so long ago. But Pius was supported by a moral power that came not only from his high office and the prayers of Christians everywhere; but from the intelligence and the spiritual grandeur of the man himself. For the Holy Father was at once a mystic dedicated to the service of God and a realist who understood the ways of ambitious men. He could use both worldly and spiritual means to combat them.

Pius's first thought was for the people of his city. As the neo-Fascists began their murderous revenge and their attacks upon the Jews, thousands of refugees poured into Vatican City, seeking the sanctuary that, as in medieval days, was to be found in the House of God.

Mostly they came at night. Their favourite entry place was near the railway station where the walls were lowest. But often when Pius looked from his window down on the great deserted Square, he would see dark figures break madly across the painted border line of his domain and flit through the shadowy colonnades to safety.

Thousands of others sought shelter in the basilicas and other buildings of the Holy See outside the Vatican walls, and no less than fifteen thousand were sheltered at Castel Gandolfo.

Though there were supposed to be rigid requirements as to identification for entry into the Papal State, Pius let it be known that his guards were not to keep too strict an accounting. No man who needed sanctuary was refused—white or black or yellow, Protestant, Catholic or Jew; it made no difference. The Pope held them in his sheltering arms.

There were many Jews. On September 28, the Chief Rabbi of Rome sought the aid of the Holy Father. The Nazis and neo-Fascists had demanded the tremendous ransom of 1,000,000 lire and one hundred pounds of gold from the Jewish residents with the threat of looting their homes and enslaving them. The Jews of Rome raised the lire, but they simply did not have that much of the precious metal. Could the Pope help them?

Pius did not hesitate. Within twenty-four hours the ransom was paid. Though he has never told how the gold was obtained, it is known that he ordered that holy vessels should be melted down to provide the funds for this most Christ-like succour of those of an alien faith.

But the golden sacrifice bought not safety, but only a respite for the Jews. Soon the methodical pogrom began again. Jewish houses and stores were smashed and looted by the neo-Fascists; Jewish families were broken up, their menfolk shipped into slavery in northern Italy and Germany; the women and children left without sustenance or shelter. Hundreds sought protection, among them Chief Rabbi Zolli himself.

Two years later, after the invader had gone and Italy was once more free, the Chief Rabbi of Rome embraced the Catholic faith.

Quite early in the occupation Hitler, furious against Italy for making terms with the Allies, decided that General Stahel was too lenient with the Romans. He replaced the Austrian with tough General Maeltzer and sent in two thousand of the Gestapo. These fanatical Nazis, who were very different from the regular German troops, went to work to round up Roman men and boys for transfer to the factories of the north. Streets and piazzas were cordoned off, and every able-bodied man and boy found in them was arrested and transported. At this point half of Rome was hiding the other half; and every night more people poured over the Vatican walls.

The Lateran Palace had some very eminent guests; among them Alcide de Gasperi, head of the Christian Democratic Party, who after the liberation was Prime Minister of Italy for many years. There was also Pietro Nenni, de Gasperi's great Socialist opponent. Despite their political antipathy, de Gasperi and Nenni became great friends during their voluntary imprisonment. However, though all the other political refugees regularly attended religious services, Nenni refused to go. "I can't," he said, "it would be too ridiculous. You see I'm a revolutionary!"

At the peak, what with all the embassies to the Holy See and the refugees, there were several thousand people living in the Vatican. Feeding them was a tremendous problem. Fortunately, part of Pius's arrangement with Kesselring and German Ambassador von Weizsächer was that the railway service to the Vatican would not be interrupted.

Through this channel food and supplies purchased by the Holy See and contributed by the faithful poured into the beleaguered city. Much of it poured out again as the Pope sent convoys of trucks to isolated parts of the Papal domains, and to relieve the distress of starving communities outside his realm.

During the early years of the war, Pope Pius had tried hard to maintain the theoretical neutrality of the Holy See, although at such times as the Nazi attack on neutral Holland and Belgium he had minced no words. But under the growing barbarity of the occupation of Rome, he scarcely bothered to pretend any more. The appearance of impartiality grew thin indeed, for Pius was hardly the man to stand aside in the battle with anti-Christ. In all ways that he could, without driving the invaders to the final step of occupying the Vatican itself, the Holy Father aided his people and the Allies.

One of these ways was the matter of Papal identity cards. These were respected by the Germans and gave the bearer immunity from persecution. The cards were issued as a matter of course to all people connected with the Holy See. But they were very easy to forge. Many thousands of Italians possessed these forgeries. The Nazis were quite aware of this and brought tremendous pressure on Vatican officials and the Pope himself to change the cards into a form less easily imitated and to tighten up on their issue. Pius blandly did nothing about it, and the exasperated Germans got the impression that he really did not care how many people held spurious but valuable safe conducts.

This could be called passive resistance, but, though it

has never been proved, there is every reason to suppose that the Pope also took a dynamic part in discomforting his oppressors. Take, for example, the activities of Monsignor Hugh O'Flaherty.

O'Flaherty is a tall, athletic Irishman, as rugged as the hills of County Cork, whence he came. Now the monsignor knew, none better, that in the chaos following the Italian surrender, many Allied prisoners-of-war had escaped from the prison camps and taken to the wooded hills that ringed the gentle fields of the Campagna. There they had been joined by many Italians escaping from the Gestapo and the neo-Fascists. Life in the hills was fine and free during the summer and the golden Italian autumn. But when winter came on, these ex-prisoners were forced to seek shelter in villages and towns. Farmers and townsmen fed and housed them. When a village got too 'hot', they built shelters for their uninvited guests in the forests, and a regular dispatch service grew up to supply them with food, cigarettes and even magazines to read.

But with tens of thousands of German troops roaming through the mountains, their situation became very precarious. So, many of these Americans and British slipped into Rome seeking the safety of numbers and the anonymity of a crowd.

That was where O'Flaherty came in. He had been one of the priests designated by the Holy Father to visit the English-speaking prisoners-of-war in the prison camps and fortresses of Italy. When they reached Rome, these men whom he had comforted made secret inquiries for their Irish friend, and the word was carried to O'Flaherty.

The first few found that the priest had not forgotten them.

He found places for them to hide and bought food and necessities for them. Others came, and O'Flaherty was worried. He was running out of funds. But he had powerful friends among the Roman nobility to whom he appealed. Led by Prince Doria, they responded bountifully with their money and services. O'Flaherty started hiring large apartments with as many as twelve rooms apiece. In a very short time the monsignor was practically the Conrad Hilton of the 'underground', with more than sixty apartments of which he was the proprietor or manager, inhabited by several hundred escapees.

He had a nerve-racking time keeping his boys under cover, for they were a reckless lot, and liked to get out and roam the streets. For the most part he managed to keep good discipline. Adventurous himself, he realised that 'the boys' needed some fresh air and exercise; so he rigged them out in disguises that varied from civilian clothes to nuns' habits and allowed them to prowl the city. One of them sat next to Marshal Kesselring at the Opera one night. He had the nerve to hand the German Commander-in-Chief his programme and ask for an autograph. Kesselring obliged.

On another occasion O'Flaherty was standing beside one of the great ladies of Rome looking out of her apartment window, when he rudely interrupted her in mid-sentence by exclaiming, "The idiot has forgotten his boots!"

The lady gasped, and O'Flaherty hastily explained: "See those two nuns crossing the piazza. They are British officers, but one of them is still wearing his service boots. They'll be picked up sure as St. Patrick converted the Irish."

Then he was off like an Olympic sprinter to get his charges under cover.

Of course, some of O'Flaherty's boys were captured; like the Englishman who underestimated his capacity for vino and insisted on singing 'Tipperary' to a wildly excited crowd in the middle of the Piazza Venezia. But none of them gave their priestly friend away. But for all those months O'Flaherty kept a knotted rope beside the window of his room to escape by in case the enemy thundered at his door.

That this very condensed account of the multifarious and highly un-neutral extra-curricular activities of the Very Reverend Monsignor O'Flaherty is true will be attested by some hundreds of grateful members of the Eighth Army and, in his more expansive moments, by Monsignor O'Flaherty himself. But how does this concern the Pope, high in his secluded study in the Vatican? How does it not? For, though the venturesome monsignor was just the fellow to dare the Gestapo's worst, and twist the swastika on Kesselring's shoulder right side out, he would never have done anything contrary to the wishes of the Holy Father. Nor would he have kept so grave an infringement of Papal neutrality a secret from the head of his Church.

One can hardly blame Nazis and neo-Fascists for being exasperated by the situation. To end it, they put all sorts of pressure on the Holy Father to leave Rome, and go to Liechtenstein for his own safety. "You have the power to imprison us," Pius told Ambassador von Weizsächer, "but you cannot persuade us to forsake our charge. We do not leave Rome!"

To emphasise their point, a little bombing raid was then organised; whether by the Nazis or the neo-Fascists was never proved, though there is strong evidence that the plane was piloted by a leading Fascist official's personal secretary.

Be that as it may, the facts are that a single plane came low over the Vatican on the night of November 5, 1943, and dropped four small bombs. One demolished the mosaic studio near the Vatican railway station. Debris and blast shattered the windows of the high cupola of St. Peter's. The other bombs fell in open spaces smashing windows of the surrounding buildings and one nearly succeeded in wrecking the Vatican radio station.

The following day a great crowd of Romans gathered in St. Peter's Square under the Pope's window, and stood there cheering him for more than two hours.

Twice more the oppressor tried to frighten off the resolute Pontiff by similar attacks. The last one came on the eve of the fifth anniversary of Pius's election to the Papal throne, March 1, 1944. Just as Pius was sitting down to his dinner he heard the roar of a low-flying plane followed by six explosions that shook the ancient walls. One of the bombs was so close that fragments fell in the Court of St. Damaso within a few feet of the outer wall of the Holy Father's apartment.

Before this, when the Nazi pressure on him to leave Rome was becoming very acute, Pius decided on an unprecedented, drastic action. On February 9, 1944, he summoned all the cardinals then in Rome to the Vatican. They awaited him in the Sistine Chapel. Pius came to them, not in splendour as he usually appeared, but walking swiftly in the simple white cassock of every day.

Very gravely he told them of the situation and of his resolve that, since he had ordered all Catholic bishops to remain at their posts, the Bishop of Rome would not leave his.

But he said, "We release you from any obligation to follow our fate. Each one of you is free to do what you think best."

Then, in that most beautiful chapel where five years before they had sworn fealty to him and kissed his foot, he absolved them from their oath. If anything should happen to him, he told them, if he were imprisoned or killed, they must gather together wherever they could and elect a new Pope.

White-faced and with tears streaming from their eyes the cardinals all refused this one command of their Pontiff; and together they pledged their faith to him once more.

When the Allies landed at Anzio, only thirty miles south of Rome, on January 21, 1944, the situation became even more stringent. Though the Germans succeeded in sealing off the beach-head, which they jeeringly called "a concentration camp where the inmates feed themselves," Italian hopes rose and the activities of the 'underground' intensified. So violent were the Romans against their oppressors that no German dared enter the crowded core of Rome, the Trastevere quarter, either by night or by day.

The Nazis took correspondingly harsher measures. For each German killed by the 'underground', ten Romans, chosen at random, were shot. When thirty-seven Germans were killed by a bomb explosion on the Via Rasella, 320 men were rounded up and taken to the caves of Domitilla on the outskirts of the city. There they were machine-gunned, and the entrance to the caves was dynamited, sealing their tombs.

Encouraged by the attitude of their Supreme Pontiff, many of the clergy took an active part in the Resistance.

The Pope had ruled that what his priests did to help the 'underground' was their private concern, which in no way compromised Papal neutrality. Though this freed them to pursue the right as they saw it, by the same token it stopped Pius from making effective protest if they were caught.

Protest he did, nevertheless, and sometimes succeeded in saving them. Not so in the case of Don Giuseppe Morosini, a young priest who was caught by the Gestapo with a stock of guns and pistols and a radio transmitter. The best grace Pius could obtain for him was permission to say Mass the morning of his execution. But Don Giuseppe and others like him had the supreme comfort of knowing that, as they faced the firing squads, the Holy Father was on his knees before his private altar, supplicating God on their behalf.

Nor were these wickednesses all that troubled Pius, for the Allies, too, gave him cause to grieve. On February 10, 1944, probably by accident, Castel Gandolfo was bombed by American planes. Five hundred refugees perished.

Then came the terrible saturation bombing of Monte Cassino, which General Clark felt was a military necessity. Weeping, the Abbot of Monte Cassino, Bishop Gregorio Diamare, came to see the Holy Father that night. Pius gave him what comfort he could, but said no word in public of his private anguish.

Meanwhile many a night was riven by the sickening blast of bursting bombs and the crack of anti-aircraft cannon as the Allies staged raid after raid on the great marshalling yards where supplies kept pouring through for Kesselring's armies.

Indeed this was a time of terrible travail for Pius, his personal Calvary. Often he felt like St. Augustine weeping in his garden, overcome by the vileness of the world and his own shortcomings until he heard the child's voice saying, "Take and read." So was Pius comforted by prayer; and he would have spent whole days on his knees had not intelligence, directing duty, forced him to spend at least twelve hours at his desk.

There was so much to do! As the Allies slowly fought their way up the Peninsula, people fleeing from the battle-fields came to Rome. It is estimated that 500,000 refugees had swelled its walls to bursting by May, 1944. Pius gave them permission to take shelter in basilicas and churches, and under the colonnades around St. Peter's Square. But at night the Gestapo-imposed curfew forced them to push into already crowded buildings, sleeping in halls and on landings.

These people faced starvation; and here Pius took vigorous action. He assembled a large fleet of motor trucks and, marking them with the Cross and the Papal colours of yellow and white on sides and roof, sent them to scour the country-side for food.

Since these convoys were respected by the Allied Air Forces the Germans used to sneak military trucks in at front and rear to gain shelter by association. The Allies soon caught on, and their airmen became quite expert at picking off the military vehicles without disrupting the Papal convoys, though inevitably some of the Pope's trucks were hit.

The first convoy brought back over 300,000 pounds of food. Pius opened soup kitchens where as many as 200,000 soup rations and 50,000 hot meals were served every day.

To finance his relief activities—the soup kitchens alone cost about $7,000 a day—the Pope organised a great "Crusade of Charity" throughout the world. In addition, all those who

applied for Papal audiences were given to understand that
the most acceptable gift they could bring the Holy Father
was food. Thousands of tons of provisions were secured in
this way.

By the end of March it became evident to the Germans that
they could hold Rome only a month or two more, and they
began to look towards their departure. On March 29, 1944,
General Kesselring declared Rome an "open city." At the
same time the Germans again urged the Pope to leave for a
safer place. To this plea Pius replied acidly, "If Rome is
really an open city, why don't *you* leave?"

The Holy Father knew that the anxiety of the Germans to
be rid of him was because they hesitated to defend Rome
while he was there. He preferred to take any personal risk,
preferred death itself, to seeing Rome made into a battlefield.
The Romans well knew how much they owed to his decision
to remain in the city. They used to say, "The Pope is our
best anti-aircraft."

On March 12, the fifth anniversary of his coronation, Pius
had appeared in public for the first time since the occupation.
Speaking to the crowd so vast that it flowed from St. Peter's
Square back across the Tiber, he asked, "How can we believe
that anyone would dare to turn Rome, this noble city which
belongs to all times and to all places . . . into a field of battle
and thus perpetuate an act as inglorious militarily as it is
abominable in the eyes of God . . . ?"

His plea had its effect, not only on the advancing Allies,
but on the Nazis themselves. Early in April, Field-Marshal
Kesselring again called on the Pope, who had at his side
Cardinal Maglione, his Secretary of State. The rock-faced

marshal was even grimmer than before, though a shade less assured. He told Pius that he, too, wished to spare the Holy City, and would not defend it. And he kept his word.

Meanwhile the whole Catholic world, indeed the whole Christian world, was bringing pressure on the Allies not to attack the city directly. Heads of the few remaining neutral nations made solemn appeals. All the American bishops joined to beseech them; and even the predominantly Protestant United States Senate urged that Rome be spared at all costs.

As the spring push of the Allied armies got under way, Pius's anxiety reached new intensity. By the end of May, the Eighth Army had reached the Alban Hills encircling the cup of the Campagna. From the terraces of the superb Villa d' Este at Tivoli and the gardens of Frascati American soldiers could see the great Dome of St. Peter's floating like an iridescent bubble against the sunset sky. And Pius from his study window could hear the booming of artillery, and see the puff ball smoke of shell-bursts at the rim of the plain.

The city was jammed with German troops, more of them than ever before, and Pius was in anguish lest Kesselring should act from desperation. But it turned out to be the concentration before the retreat.

Rome was like a dead city, those first days of June. There was no gas, no electricity. Newspapers could not be published. Food was scarce and even water, the gay and carelessly flowing water of Roman fountains, was cut off. There was no transport of any sort. A feeling of lawlessness was oppresive in the air that any spark might explode.

Late on June 2, 1944, the Germans started to leave. All

that night Pius heard the rumble of tanks and heavy vehicles heading north. June 3 was strangely silent, as the artillery in the hills stopped firing and the battle noises ceased. The long snakes of the German columns crawled out of the northern gates, and the Americans and British stood by their silent guns and watched them go.

The Roman people watched them, too. From crowded pavements and cafes they stared at their former conquerors moving wearily, heavy-eyed and shoddy; on foot or in stolen vehicles, in horse-drawn wagons, some even pulling hand-carts.

The previous September they had come arrogantly in their new trucks and tanks, machine-guns pointing. Now they looked strained and justly frightened, for they were afraid the Roman people, the *populus Romanus* whom even Ceasar had feared, would rise and rend them. But the Pope had begged his people not to start a slaughter by seeking revenge; and they obeyed him.

It was late the following evening, June 4, that the first Allied patrols entered the city, slipping like shadows up the pitch dark streets, cautiously with guns at the ready. Soon there was no more need for caution. By early morning all Rome was in the streets, cheering madly, throwing showers of roses, whose petals clung to trucks and guns and roaring tanks. The roadway was pink with petals as the Americans, throwing toffee and cigarettes to the laughing, singing people, marched towards the Porta Pinciana. Women swarmed over their jeeps and trucks and even tried to climb on the tanks, giving the men bottles of wine and getting heartily kissed. As French troops passed along the Via dell' Impero, the Romans recognised them and yelled "Vive la France!"

177

The British, smiling and nonchalant, moved up the Via Nazionale and the Via Ludovisi, led by Scottish pipers with swinging kilts. Across the Tiber, Pius heard the wonderful wild skirling of the pipes and smiled for the first time in weeks.

Later that Sunday it seemed that everybody in Rome tried to get into St. Peter's Square. Hastily borrowed trucks spilling over with teen-agers and flowers tore around the city, their occupants shouting, "Come to St. Peter's!" The Piazza was jammed beyond anything seen before. All the bells of Rome pealed in deafening clangour so that the vibrations seemed to come up from the pavements through your toes and course joyously through your body.

Suddenly they all stopped and there was a complete stunning silence. The windows giving on to the balcony of the great Church opened, and Pius in his simple white cassock walked out alone, and stood looking down on his people with brimming eyes.

When he could speak, he said, "In the days just past we trembled for Rome. Today we give thanks to God, that both contending armies have collaborated to preserve the Eternal City."

Then, once again, he gave the blessing, "to the city and the world."

A few days later General Mark Clark came to pay his respects to the Holy Father. He wore battle dress, not nearly so fine as Kesselring's elegant uniform. Though his long, lean face was worn and eroded with care, his eyes were gentle. Almost the first thing he said to the Holy Father was an apology. "I am afraid you have been disturbed by the noise of my tanks," he said. "I am sorry."

That wonderful, warm, happy smile lit Pius's face. "General," he said, "any time you come to liberate Rome, you can make just as much noise as you like."

*

CHAPTER SEVENTEEN

"SAVE THE CHILDREN"

THE tide of war receded rapidly from Rome, as the German armies retreated up the ancient Aurelian Way towards Florence and the North; and the armed might of America and England flowed after them, past the lichen-covered walls in a thunderous wave of sound. So Rome breathed again, but it was a breath of pain and privation, searing the lungs and hunger-swollen stomachs of the children; making the old wish to die, and darkening the dreams of everyone. Throughout modern times Rome had often seemed more like a museum than a city; now it appeared likely to become a gigantic mausoleum.

Pius suffered deeply for the afflicted; and in all his waking hours thought of the unwanted orphans of the war. He pictured in his mind the frantic searching of garbage cans for food; the small bodies huddled in doorways during the long cold hours of the night; the shameless transactions of the lively days. Even in the night, he told his intimates, he saw the eyes of the forgotten children, furtive, defenceless, or glazed by hopelessness. So he mobilised all the resources of the Papacy to alleviate their misery.

Relief work was intensified. The number of ration stations was doubled; for, even though the main administration of material supplies had been taken over by the Allies, the Vatican carried a tremendous burden. In 1944, 3,500,000 food rations were distributed from the Vatican free kitchens. This was increased to a total of 29,000,000 in 1945. And in 1946 approximately 41,000,000 free rations were distributed. Even as late as 1947, the Pope fed an average of 250,000 people a day. Always the Holy Father thought first of the children. On some occasions he had 50,000 children eating at the Vatican.

Nor did Pius confine his Crusade of Charity to Rome. He sent his convoys of yellow and white trucks filled with food and medical supplies following hard on the heels of the advancing Allies. They were commanded by priests who spoke several languages. In his orders to them Pius stressed again the universality of the Church. There was to be no discrimination, but all, of whatever nation or race or creed, who needed help were to be given it alike.

In addition to the motorcades, freight carloads of food were sent to all parts of Italy.

Nor did Pius's concern stop at the borders of Italy. As the Allied armies crashed into Austria and Germany during the final bitter stages of the war, the Papal motorcades followed them into the heart of the defeated countries. Their goal was the concentration camps. In over two hundred of these cesspools of misery, the Papal emissaries distributed 2,500,000 parcels of food and clothing to the starving inmates.

But Pius realised that this was not enough. World-wide help was needed to repair the world-wide ravages of global war. In 1946 he began a "Save the Children Campaign," with an encyclical addressed to people everywhere whose homes had not been destroyed and whose children were safe.

In a matter of days an avalanche of gifts began to pile up in the historic courtyards of the Vatican. Soon these overflowed, and other buildings had to be hired to house the welcome crates of food and clothing. America sent thirty million tins of food. Even England, itself rationed to the edge of malnutrition, depleted her small stocks of food to give to those more desperately in want.

Almost as fast as they came in, the supplies were sent off to the children of despair in Poland, China, Belgium, Burma, Greece, and to Germany and Austria, and wherever war had struck. With the food and clothing went devoted men and women who dedicated themselves to the work of rescue and rehabilitation.

Pius did not limit his concern to children, though they came first. He was very conscious of the plight of millions of displaced persons who were still in concentration camps or thronging the roads of Europe; and of the prisoners of war still held in prison camps. In a broadcast the day after the armistice was signed, he petitioned the Allied commands to release the latter, saying over the radio: "We know that the letter of international law does not impose the obligation to free the prisoners of war before the signing of peace. But the spiritual and moral deeds of the prisoners and of their families necessitates that we should bring an end to their confinement, and of concentration camps of every kind."

The Holy Father allocated millions of lire to the assistance of displaced persons. At least 650,000 families were repatriated and rehabilitated entirely at the expense of the Holy See. Meanwhile hospital trains flying the Papal colours travelled the dilapidated railways of Europe collecting and caring for over 25,000 sick people.

Despite all its material misery, Rome was a far happier city after the Germans left. For one thing the Holy Father threw his doors open again to the people, who were received in large public and smaller private audiences. Pius was especially happy to see soldiers of the Allied armies. American generals and privates in hob-nailed boots and battle-stained uniforms crowded the great Hall of Benediction every day. Pius had ordered that all regulations of ceremonial dress be relaxed, even the time-honoured rule that women must be veiled and clothed from head to foot in black. So American WACs in baggy trousers mingled with their masculine comrades in the crowded rooms.

The first time Pius received a group of American soldiers he was greatly distressed by their apparently aloof attitude. "Why do they act so coldly," he asked. "Do they not like me?"

Someone explained, "They are not cold, but in awe of you. The Italians know you well, and are at ease in your presence; but to these men you are an object of such reverence that they cannot be natural."

As soon as he heard this, Pius set out to remedy the situation, moving among the soldiers, laughing with them and making little jokes. The ice melted with a rush, as awe was replaced by friendly admiration.

Many Americans besides the soldiers came to Rome during the last year of war, and almost all of them asked for and received audiences with the Holy Father. A delegation of United States congressmen and senators arrived just before Christmas, 1944. One of them was Clare Boothe Luce, congresswoman from Connecticut. Pius recognised her, having received her once before, though that time she was swathed in black, her golden hair hidden by a black lace mantilla, and now she wore only a black silk suit. Seeing by her lovely, troubled face, that she had something on her mind, the Holy Father gave her leave to speak.

"What I must tell you," she said, speaking very slowly and precisely, "is that we women have less faith in keeping the peace by military might than our men seem to. We believe that justice, charity and love must be the foundation of true peace."

Pius was happy to hear a member of the American Congress speak thus closely to his own thoughts, though he would have added, "Faith in God." And so would Mrs. Luce at a somewhat later date.

Another distinguished visitor whom Pius received in private audience shortly after the war was Winston Churchill. The great British Prime Mininster told the Holy Father of Joseph Stalin's cynical question at the Yalta Conference, "How many divisions has the Pope?"

"When you see Our son Joseph again," Pius said a little grimly, "tell him that he will meet Our divisions in heaven."

The war in Europe ended officially on May 8, 1945. The following day, Pius talked over the radio to the world of the peace he hoped would follow. In this address he implored the leaders of the victorious nations "to create a better Europe, a better universe, based upon the love of a Son of God the Father; steadfastness to His commands; and acknowledgment of human dignity, and, above all, the holy principle of the equality of rights of all people, nations and states, great and small, weak and strong. . . . The war brought everywhere discord, hatred, indifference. If our world wishes to regain true peace, falsehood and anger and bitterness must disappear; and truth and love must take their place."

By way of emphasising his personal adherence to this doctrine, Pius announced in his Christmas allocution to the Sacred College that he would soon create thirty-two new cardinals. Irrespective of race or nationality he would raise to the dignity of Prince of the Church men from countries great and small in five continents. Never before in history had so many cardinals been created at one consistory. The new cardinals came from England, France, Spain, Germany, Italy, Poland, Hungary, Holland, Canada, Argentina, Brazil, Chile, Peru, Cuba, Syria, Austria, Africa, China, and the United States. One of the four he created from the States was his old friend and fellow-worker, Archbishop Francis Spellman.

The consistory was held on February 18, 1946. Usually on these great ceremonial occasions, Pius in his white, gold-encrusted robes seemed like a frail figure from a stained-glass window, aloof and exalted in his mystic conception of his spiritual rôle. But that day, as he observed the freshly created cardinals, splendid in their new crimson robes, he sensed that many of them were awed, almost crushed by their new dignity, and in his gentle courtesy he set out to make them feel at ease. So, as he moved among them, placing the birettas on golden heads and white, on kinky black hair or straight dark Asian locks, he whispered little confidences to them that made them smile in all their solemnity; and he, too, smiled heart-warmingly at them.

One of the cardinals created that day was Count von Galen, Bishop of Münster. Because, throughout the most stringent days of war, he had defied Hitler and the whole

Nazi mechanism of repression, he was known affectionately as 'The Lion of Münster'. As this giant of a man knelt before the Holy Father, Pius whispered in his ear, "God bless Germany!"

When each cardinal had his Red Hat, Pius spoke to them and all their colleagues with the solemn fervour of his passionate belief. "Now that the world war is over," he said, "we shall have the consolation of seeing around us members of the Sacred College from all five continents. And so Rome will be seen, as she truly is, the Eternal and Universal City, the *Caput Mundi,* the head of the world, and the world will know that all men are citizens of this city. We have wished that the greatest possible number of peoples be represented so that the universality of the Church be a living picture in the minds of all."

Pius made his point still more clear when on February 28 he received the Diplomatic Corps. His tall white figure seemed to shine transcendentally as he stood surrounded by the cardinals in their flowing red silk robes facing the diplomats, in their gold-laced uniforms. "The fact that you are here," he said, "indicates that you are in accord with that which from the day we were elected, we have continually held up to the world. . . . We know that your desire is to co-operate with us in the rebuilding of society and establishing order through justice and love."

Then Pius pressed the view he held most strongly, that of the supranationality of the Church, "which does not suppress the different characteristics of the different nations, but allows each one its place in the harmony of the whole."

However, Pius did not include all forms of government in his tolerance. In his Christmas speech of 1945, he had warned of the dangers attending the intrusion of Communist Russia into European affairs, saying that, "The totalitarian state is diametrically opposed to the principles of democracy . . . and is a constant source of the danger of war. The future peace must banish every opportunity of waging an offensive war, and every mode of aggression, but totalitarianism does not permit this."

Thus Pius, nearly a year before Winston Churchill's Iron Curtain speech, publicly prophesied the danger of Communist aggression.

Though the coming of peace temporarily eased the Holy Father's anxieties, it can be seen that it hardly lessened the amount of work he had to do. However, it gave him one great relaxation. During the war he had resolutely refused to leave Rome for so much as an hour, even during the infernal Roman summer. Now he felt that he could go again to his beloved Castel Gandolfo.

Castel Gandolfo is a tiny town that long ago attached itself to the walls of the medieval fortress which guarded its mountain top. Indeed, the entrance to the town was once the main gate of the castle. It has a single large square, one side of which is the high wall with massive gates that lead to the central courtyard of the Pope's villa. It is the focal point of a few narrow, twisting streets that begin nowhere and end in the square. The little domain curls itself around the lip of an ancient volcanic crater which underground springs have turned into a lovely lake, so sheltered by the thickly wooded walls of the crater that it is a flawless mirror for the summer sky.

The castle itself was originally built by the Gandulfi family about 1150 A.D. as their mountain stronghold. The present palace, built in the sixteenth century by Maderna, is a rather large Italian country house, and its lovely chapel was designed by Bernini. The Holy See bought it in 1623. From then until 1870 it was continuously used as the summer residence of the Popes. But when King Victor Emmanuel took over the Papal States, Pius IX shut himself up in the Vatican and refused to go to Castel Gandolfo, even though the Italian Government guaranteed it to the Vatican. After the signing of the Lateran Pact in 1929, Pope Pius XI once again spent his summers in the refreshing air of his private hilltop. Until the war Pius XII followed his example.

It is likely that Pius loves Castel Gandolfo more than any other Pope. It reminds him of the wonderful peaceful days he spent at Onano when he was young. Indeed, he was so impatient to reach it that, as the black Papal Cadillac passed through the gates of Rome's Aurelian Wall to the Via Appia and the open Campagna, he always pulled out his watch and noted the time. If the drive of 17.4 miles was made in eighteen minutes he was well pleased; but if it took nineteen minutes he gently chided his driver, Angelo Stoppa.

His love of speed is one of the contradictory characteristics of this mystic-modern Pope. Speaking to participants in the second world congress of the International Road Federation in October, 1955, Pius said, "Individuals, societies, and nations must enter a universal race for greater and greater speed to the glory of God. . . . Dispensaries, teachers and missionaries must now travel by speedway, bringing health of body and soul faster than ever before. . . . He would be a heartless man who opposed building speedways. . . .

"But," Pius added, "while speed there must be to the glory

of God, and it is essential ever to increase it, it must be accompanied by courtesy, which is in the Christian tradition, and prudence, which is one of the seven virtues. Those long lines of cars driving along speedways must be impelled by the desire to serve, not to dominate."

The Pope went even further in talking to a group of young Italian motor-scooter riders, and his words denote a certain out-of-this-worldliness in his attitude towards the vexatious Vespa. To them he said, "Those who complain of the noise you make, do they ever think that your speed may take you to church in time for Mass, or that you may be rushing a sick person to the hospital? Be patient with those who abuse you."

Due largely to Pius's encouragement, more than 30,000 Italian priests now use motor scooters.

Once at Castel Gandolfo, the tempo of life slowed wonderfully for Pius. He still transacted all his regular business, and held frequent public audiences which packed the big courtyard of the Villa so closely with cheering humanity that, though a person might faint from emotion, he could not fall down. But there was also time for contemplation, for long walks in the superb gardens built on the terraced sides of the old volcano's cone.

There were a hundred and twenty acres of gardens for Pius to ramble through, crossed by broad avenues lined with ilex trees and by curving gravelled walks. There were walled rose gardens, and flower-filled terraces that seemed to be suspended in air. Hidden in the wilder sections were the remains of ancient Roman villas—broken but still lovely marble columns and bits of finely worked mosaics.

Best of all Pius loved to stand on one of the terraces listening to the crystal murmur of the many fountains and looking at the magnificent view: the mirror of the lake reflecting the dark greens of the woods and the warm blue of the sky, and away to the north-east the Campagna spreading to the soft foothills and angry peaks of the Sabine hills; and to the west the flat, productive plain flowing in a golden tide to the faint shimmer of blue that was the Tyrrhenian Sea.

Though Pius was still surrounded by his archaicly uniformed Papal Guard, and his colourful suite of cardinals, bishops and monsignori, even the public aspects of his life were less formal than at the Vatican, and his private audiences became extremely informal indeed. One such was the occasion on which he received the Harlem Globe Trotters, a basketball team who were touring Europe playing matches and giving exhibitions of their skill. They had expressed a wish to see the Pope; so Pius received them in the great hall of his villa. After greeting them, he walked around among the players showing by his conversation that he had read of their victories in the sports pages of the newspapers. "I am only sorry I could never see you play," he said.

The boys looked at each other and the spacious hall. Pius sensed their thoughts. "Why not now?" he asked.

Then and there the Globe Trotters went into their famous ring formation. One of them produced a ball, and they began passing it around the circle with incredible velocity, at the same time whistling their theme song, 'Sweet Georgia Brown', and clapping their hands to the beat. Pius laughed and applauded with pleasure, and the players noticed that the Pope's slipper was tapping out the rhythm.

Afterwards they lined up in two rows to have their picture

taken with the Holy Father, who stood in the middle of the front row. Those at the back asked the Pope if he would mind posing again with them in the front row. "Not at all," said Pius smiling. "I have learned that Americans always want 'just one more'."

Though the end of the war had relieved the Pope's greatest anxiety and the quiet days at Castel Gandolfo had refreshed his spirit, it was a temporary respite. From the signing of the truce, indeed even before the Yalta Conference, things began to go badly.

Pius had welcomed the Atlantic Charter as an expression of the ideals of mankind which he shared with its makers. But as victory for the Allies came closer, those ideals seemed to fade; and in the let-down after the firing ceased, it seemed to Pius that they were forgotten altogether. It rapidly became evident that the armistice was to be followed by no true peace, but only by what Pius called *'il dopoguerra'*, the aftermath of war.

The failure of the Paris Conference of 1946 confirmed his pessimism, and in his Christmas message that year he said sadly, "Humanity, just emerging from the horrors of a brutal war, looks with stupor upon the gulf between the hopes of yesterday, and the actions of today. . . . When the Atlantic Charter was first announced it was received with the acclamations of mankind. . . . (But) the Four Freedoms, once so enthusiastically hailed, now seem but a shadow and a mockery of the intentions of those who formulated them."

Indeed, Pius felt that all the ideals he had shared with the Allied leaders, with Churchill and with Franklin Roosevelt, whose voice had now been silenced by death, were being betrayed. Worse still, over sixty million Catholics in countries such as Hungary, Czechoslovakia, the Baltic States, Poland, and a dozen others, had been handed over to the Communists, who were vigorously pursuing a policy of 'forcible conversion' to the doctrine of Marxism and the god-state.

Though, as an experienced diplomat, Pius must have realised the difficulty of ejecting the Russians from countries which their vast armies had conquered, as the father of these people, which he truly felt himself to be, he could only sorrow for their fate and indignantly reject the plea of practical necessity.

Indeed, he was almost as concerned for the state of the Protestants and Moslems in the enslaved nations. For they, too, were being denied the right to worship God.

The final blow to the melancholy state of mankind was the invention of the atomic bomb, that ultimate weapon of indiscriminate destruction.

Viewing so dark a future, Pius might well have been tempted to follow a not un-Christian precedent, and withdraw from the struggle into the mystic isolation of a holy hermit. Mystic he surely was; but a fighting mystic, who would never cease to battle against evil while life remained. So he prepared to throw all his personal strength and the great moral powers of his Church, and the spiritual force of his heavenly divisions into this Armageddon for the souls of men.

*

CHAPTER EIGHTEEN

THE FIGHT AGAINST

COMMUNISM

THE battle which Pius had foreseen as early as 1944, when the Communists moved into Poland, was soon joined in every country under Russia's influence. For Stalin aimed to be the supreme ruler of his subjects' religion as well as their politics, and would brook no other Pope than he; while Communism, which is a cradle-to-grave blueprint for its people—a sort of religion without a god—could not comfortably co-exist with any church founded on Christian principles.

So in all the countries that had fallen to Communism, which included most of eastern Europe, Stalin began the systematic extirpation of all religion, with special venom directed against the Catholic Church. Pius was reminded of another invasion of Europe by the Mohammedan Turks, who had also reached the gates of Vienna. But this one was far worse; for Mohammedans at least believe in God!

Though the process of de-Christianisation did not begin simultaneously in all the Iron Curtain countries, the pattern was sadly similar in each. First, there was an outburst of anti-religion in the captive press. Then the Pope himself was attacked as an ally of Western imperialists and local reactionaries. After a period of ideological softening-up, anti-religious and anti-clerical laws were promulgated. Religious institutions were deprived of their incomes; convents and monasteries forcibly disbanded; religious schools closed; priests forbidden to exercise their ministerial duties outside of the church walls; and bishops were so restricted in their pastoral duties that they could not fulfil their functions without being arrested.

That was the devilish ingenuity of the plan. The first attack was not made on religion; but on the clergy, who were smeared as spies, traitors and tools of reaction.

Though he had expected the enmity of Communism for the Church, Pius was amazed by the ferocity of the personal attacks on him. To John McKnight, author of *The Papacy,* he cried in anguish, "Why are the Russians as they are? . . . Why do they say the things about me that they do?"

Like the Pope, the Communists paid special attention to the children. Unlike him, they sought to twist their minds away from God; to turn them from love to hatred even of their own kin, encouraging them to act as informers against their parents, teaching them to sing blasphemous songs, and deliberately corrupting them spiritually, morally and even sexually. As news of these actions reached Pius he was torn between helpless anguish and holy rage.

Because the catalogue of Communist crimes against religion is so long and so dismally familiar, there is neither space nor reason here to describe the events in each country, or to tell of all the measures by which the Holy Father sought to defend his Church and his children. A few of the more outrageous incidents will suffice.

Of these the first happened in Yugoslavia, while the Communist Dictator Tito was still closely allied with Stalin. As soon as Tito came to power he began to persecute, not only Catholics, but communicants of the Orthodox Church, Jews, and Moslems as well.

In 1945, immediately after the Nazis were forced out of Yugoslavia, Pius sent the American Bishop Joseph P. Hurley to Belgrade as Nuncio to try to establish normal diplomatic relations. The bishop had been there only a matter of months when the Yugoslavian Government announced that they had proof of an understanding between the Vatican and General Mikhailovitch, who had led the anti-Communist resistance and whom Tito tried and executed on a fictitious charge of collaborating with the Nazis.

Of course Pius denied the ridiculous charge; but Communist logic carried things even further. In September, 1946, Archbishop Aloysius Stepinac, Catholic Primate of Yugoslavia, was tried on charges of treasonable association with the enemy. The Pope publicly pointed out how illogical the charges were, since it was admitted by all that Stepinac had personally saved literally thousands of Jews and Moslems as well as Christians from Nazi concentration camps.

Of course the Pope's logic had no effect on the result of the trial. Stepinac was sentenced to sixteen years' hard labour; and Hurley was forced to leave the country.

But Stepinac was lucky after all. By 1949 Vatican statisticians reckoned that some four hundred Yugoslavian priests had been put to death, three hundred more imprisoned, and ninety-odd had just disappeared.

What happened in Hungary was far worse. Ever since his mission to the International Eucharistic Congress there in 1938, Pius had had a particularly warm affection for the Hungarians. As the Iron Curtain clanked down on that country, he recalled the glorious scenes of the Congress: the beautiful Eucharistic procession of boats on the Danube, and the spontaneous joy of the people in their faith. Because of these memories he sorrowed more keenly for them, perhaps, than for other peoples he did not know as well. To fortify their faith and encourage them steadfastly to resist the false prophets of deliberate demoralisation, he beamed a special broadcast to the Hungarians and sent them a beautiful, ancient image of the Holy Virgin.

Naturally, the Pope's counter-offensive against Stalinism enraged the Hungarian Communists still further. Indeed, it led them to an action so excessive that later even they tacitly admitted that it had been a mistake. This was the arrest, brain-washing and imprisonment of Joseph Cardinal Mindszenty, Primate of Hungary.

In 1946, as the Communist campaign against the Church went into high gear, Pius had raised Mindszenty to the dignity of Prince of the Church. This was partly to give him greater prestige to combat them, and partly in recognition of his previous services and sufferings for the Faith. For Mindszenty had been so actively anti-Nazi during the war that he had been imprisoned without trial for several months. When he was finally brought before a Nazi court, the prosecutor asked for the death sentence; but this was refused. Ironically, Russian troops found Mindszenty in jail and set him free.

From 1946 onward, the cardinal was the biggest thorn in

the side of Hungarian Communism. He publicly protested every law designed to abrogate the rights of religion; and resolutely refused to collaborate or even acquiesce in the godless designs of the Government. He succeeded in stirring the consciousness and conscience of the Hungarian people. That was the unpardonable crime.

As Pius learned from reliable witnesses, and later described to a consistory of cardinals, this is what happened.

On a December midnight in 1948, a covey of police cars surrounded the cardinal's house just opposite Budapest. He heard the crunch of jack-boots on the gravel drive, the crash as the front door was smashed open. Then he was surrounded by police with drawn guns.

It was a familiar scene to the cardinal—the only difference was that Red Stars had replaced the Swastikas on the soldiers' uniforms. He dressed quietly, and spoke a few comforting words to his old mother, who stood trembling in the doorway of her room. Then he stepped into a police car and was driven with wailing sirens to the headquarters of the political police.

The Communists literally threw the book at Mindszenty, charging him with every crime they could think of—treason; plotting to overthrow the government and set up a monarchy; shady financial dealings in black market dollars; and spying on behalf of the United States!

To prove their case, the prosecutors forged the cardinal's signature to hundreds of documents; they mysteriously produced letters; and induced the Minister of Finance to perjure himself by producing phony evidence of black market dealings. But all this was not enough. To justify imprisoning a Prince of the Church they needed an air-tight case. So they went to work on the cardinal.

What Mindszenty went through is familiar to everyone who can read or watch a moving picture of Communist methods of bloodless torture. For days and weeks without let-up under the glaring lights, relays of inquisitors pounded questions at him. But the cardinal was made of sterner stuff than many who gave way; and he had his faith to uphold him. Though he fell unconscious several times during the interrogations, no amount of psychological torture could break him. So, during one of his black-outs, the Communists resorted to their mind-sapping drugs. Only then did the cardinal 'confess'.

However, the Communists might as well have spared their trouble, and just condemned Mindszenty out of hand. For virtually nobody in the free world believed in Mindszenty's self-incrimination. Instead they accepted Pius's ringing denunciation of the trial as rigged, and his description of what had been done to the cardinal. Such was the horror of Christians, Jews and people of all other religions at seeing a godly man thus deliberately debased, that it is quite probable that the Communists would have had a much less violent reaction if they had executed the cardinal that first night.

The tale of persecution in Yugoslavia and Hungary was repeated, though somewhat less horribly, in every country that the Russian Army controlled. In all of them Pius was deeply concerned, backing the clergy and exhorting the people to stand firm. For all of them he seemed to suffer in his person, as though the physical and psychological wounds of his children were transmitted to him. Indeed, he felt this to be quite literally true.

Though his greatest weapons in the Crusade against Communism were spiritual, Pius also used every technique of the skilled diplomat. During those years, he virtually redoubled the number of people he saw in private audiences; people of every race and creed to whom he used whatever argument would appeal most to them. Finally the Pope went into politics.

The Italian elections of 1948 were regarded as a crisis in the Communists' hitherto unsuccessful attempt to win countries not occupied by their armies. Some of the leading Italian journalists on both sides were prophesying that the Reds would win control of the Italian legislature. Everyone knew that if once they did there would be no second chance for democracy in Italy. So great was the danger that Pius felt that he could not stand aside, even though it meant breaking the spirit if not the letter of the Lateran Pact by which the Vatican had agreed not to interfere in governmental affairs.

Through more than 300 bishops and 125,000 prelates and nearly 5,000,000 members of Catholic Action, Pius conducted what has been described as a brilliant political campaign against the Italian Communist Party.

Finally, shortly before the election, the people of Rome were summoned to St. Peter's Square. They came in numbers estimated at hundreds of thousands. To them the Holy Father, in the white and gold vestments of his sacred office, spoke from the familiar portico. His words were carried by loudspeakers to the farthest tributaries of the crowd extending beyond the Tiber and up the Corso Vittorio Emanuele; and by radio to all Italy and the world.

It was no kindly Father blessing his city and the world

that Italians heard that day, nor the saintly mystic who was their Supreme Pontiff. It was a fighting Christian pleading for the cause in which he passionately believed; pleading with all the fiery oratory of a leader of men, the impassioned eloquence of a Savonarola dedicating Florence long ago to the Kingdom of Jesus Christ. No man who heard him could doubt that now, indeed, "The great hour of Christian conscience has come."

The Communists were routed at the polls. Sceptical John McKnight, author of *The Papacy,* who makes doubting Thomas seem like a fanatic by comparison, in his chapter on 'The Papacy and Communism' almost reluctantly states, "Perhaps as much as any one man, Pacelli was the architect of the victory of the anti-Communist forces in this vital election."

It is almost incredible that Pius's frail physique was able to withstand the strain he put upon it during the years of war and the *'dopoguerra'*. The innumerable audiences all day long; the long hours of the religious ceremonies; the periods of personal devotions, and the multiplicity of executive decisions he had to make—for he had been his own Secretary of State since Maglione died in 1944—made the Pope's day more onerous than that of any other head of state. Possibly over the years it was more strenuous than that of any other person in the world.

It was indeed an eighteen-hour day, lasting from six-thirty in the morning until long after midnight with only the brief break of his after-luncheon rest. Physical stamina alone could not carry such a load. Even the most doubting are obliged to attribute Pius's endurance to something beyond the mere mechanics of bodily strength. The spirit indeed is greater than the flesh.

There is a charming anecdote of the Holy Father at this time, sitting alone at the desk in his study, working even later than usual. His small apartment, even the whole great palace, was wrapped in complete silence. But for companionship in his lonely vigil Pius had released his favourite goldfinch, Gretel.

She fluttered about the room from the curtain pole to the Pope's shoulder. Finally she landed on the papers before him. He gently shooed her away. She swooped around the room, but instead of finding her familiar place on his shoulder, she fluttered down on the desk again. Five times the Holy Father sent her away, and each time she came back, making it impossible for him to work.

The last time he smiled wearily at her and said, "I understand. You are quite right."

Then he put her back in her cage, drew the curtain over it, and went to his devotions, and to bed.

*

CHAPTER NINETEEN

A POPE'S DAY

In the late forties, before his illness, when the disturbances of war were well in the past, the Pope's life had become channelled in an active but circumscribed routine. Of course, from the moment he became Pope, Eugenio Pacelli's travels ended for good. Though, since the signing of the Lateran Pact in 1929, the Pontiff could no longer be thought of as 'The Prisoner of the Vatican', his longest trip beyond its walls was the seventeen miles to Castel Gandolfo, and most of his life was spent in the Apostolic Palace.

No man knows the origin of the Vatican, but there is evidence that some kind of palace stood on its site at the time of the Emperor Constantine. When Charlemagne came to Rome for his coronation by Pope Leo the Great in A.D. 800, he is recorded to have stayed in a palace adjoining St. Peter's. The present Vatican is a rather haphazard collection of buildings because of additions made through the centuries, but the main part of it was built in the fourteenth and fifteenth centuries. The Palace contains over ten thousand rooms and halls and nine hundred and ninety-seven stairways, thirty of which are secret. Besides the Pope's personal quarters and his state reception rooms, there are many apartments tucked away in this palatial maze in which live cardinals, monks, the families of secular employees and a few nuns.

Vatican City, of which the palace occupies the greater part, has its own railway station on a siding which links up with the main rail network of Italy. There is a real iron curtain that can be dropped to shut off the siding. Vatican City's newspaper is *L'Osservatore Romano,* which the Pope's grandfather founded at the direction of Pius IX, and its Sunday edition *L'Osservatore della Domenica.* The Vatican State has a fire department, a police force and an army—the Pope's guards. Its national anthem was written by Gounod. As evidence that all who live there are not without sin, there are two jails.

The Palace gardens, which are the only open ground in this independent state, are rather small, but finely planted. Flowers bloom all the year round, the mown grass is always green, and many kinds of blossoming shrubs and exotic trees give variety to the scene, which is enhanced by splashing fountains. Many lovely little shrines are hidden away in unexpected corners.

Beautiful as it is, the Pope's physical world is decidedly confined. Pius X did not like it. Coming as he did from the wide valleys and abrupt hills of the north, he felt cabined and cribbed within its smallness, and often stood looking over the walls with sorrowful eyes. Pius XI must have felt the imprisonment even more, for Achille Ratti had been a noted mountain climber. But if Eugenio Pacelli, world traveller, was disturbed by his confinement he showed no sign of it.

Out of all the wealth of treasure-filled rooms, Pope Pius

XII had chosen the same small apartment as his predecessor. It consisted of two floors. The top one was the Pope's private flat. It was situated on the third storey of the Vatican at the corner overlooking St. Peter's Square and the city of Rome. There was a dining-room, bedroom, bathroom, a study, a small chapel and a few rooms for his personal attendants.

All his life Pius had been simple, frugal and ascetic. The furnishings of his rooms reflected his taste. In the bedroom was a plain walnut bed, a utilitarian little dressing-table with a mirror and a small desk piled with papers. The walls were starkly bare, their only decoration a crucifix and a picture of the Madonna.

Beside this monastic cell, the dining-room seemed almost luxurious. In the middle was a round mahogany dining table covered by a lace centrepiece on which was a crystal vase of flowers. Around the table were four cane-backed chairs with seats upholstered in red velvet. There was a small side table against one wall, supporting brass candelabra and a posy of flowers. Between the door and the single lace-curtained window was a china cabinet, with a few ceramics behind glass doors. There was also a radio on a mahogany stand.

The only touch of magnificence was the beautifully veined, highly polished marble floor. But the room was full of song, supplied by four cages of birds, one in the window bay, two hanging from brackets, and one resting on a long mahogany table. The latter was the home of the Holy Father's favourite goldfinch, Gretel. She was seldom at home, for the Pope loved to have her flying around the apartment. Gretel watched him shave with his electric razor, and perched on his shoulder at mealtimes. American Ambassador Clare Boothe Luce once asked him what he did for fun, and he replied fondly, "I have my little goldfinch."

Until his serious illness in 1954 Eugenio Pacelli had never changed the strenuously ascetic way of his life. At six every morning he would get out of bed, and, moving to the window overlooking the almost empty square and the jumbled roof-tops of Rome, he would stand and pray for a moment, and linger to watch the ever-recurring miracle of awakening day.

Next he did the morning exercises by which since his sickly youth he had kept his body in trim. For ten minutes he pedalled a stationary bicycle or strengthened his arms with a spring-loaded apparatus. When that was done he took a shower—cold except in the bitterest weather; and then shaved.

By a few minutes past seven he was dressed, and went to his private chapel, where, after passing twenty minutes in meditative prayer, he put on the vestments laid out for him and celebrated Mass. His server would be his valet, Giovanni Stefanori. A few nuns from the German-Swiss Order of the Holy Cross of Metzingen, headed by Mother Pasqualina, who kept house for him, would be his congregation.

After that the nuns served him breakfast in the dining-room—coffee and milk, a piece of bread and sometimes a little fruit. His day's work began there, for he read official papers as he drank his coffee.

At ten minutes to nine the Pope went down the private stairway to the second floor. Passing through the fine library he would greet his two archivists, or secretaries, Father

Lieber and Father Hendrich of the Jesuit Order, and go into his private office. It was a big room, with three windows from which the heavy draperies had been pulled back exposing curtains of white silk-net. Chairs upholstered in crimson damask were set ready to receive his visitors; and his large walnut desk was piled high with stacks of documents. There was a gold and white telephone on the desk and little boxes of medals and rosaries which he would give to everyone who came to see him.

As he sat at his desk, Pius faced the book-cases covered with soft gold draperies that lined the wall. He would run through the official papers hastily to see if any needed immediate attention. At exactly one minute to nine, he would press the bell button to inform the attendant monsignori that he was ready to receive the first of his visitors.

They were sure to be ready and waiting, for the Pope was noted for his punctuality and had a strict timetable for the day. However, the schedule would break down when something happened that touched his heart.

It got all askew one day when one of the chamberlains happened to mention the story of a woman who had come to Rome with her young son who was so hideously deformed that people shuddered and turned away when they saw him.

"Why do you tell me this story?" Pius asked.

The chamberlain, obviously embarrassed, said, "The woman asked for an audience, but it does not really concern you as it was refused her."

"The sufferings of people concern me greatly," the Holy Father said, and motioned the chamberlain out.

Then he picked up the telephone, and ordered a car to be sent immediately for the mother and child, and told his attendants that he would receive no one until they came.

When they arrived, the Pope took the boy in his arms and asked the mother what she had done. "Doctors could do nothing," she answered, "so I took him to Lourdes, but no miracle was given us."

"And then?" asked Pius.

"My son wanted to come to Rome to see you. We do not expect a miracle, only the assurance that God is with us."

Pius gave her that faith with all his heart. Then he blessed her and the boy in his arms; and they went away comforted.

Usually the first business of the Pope's day had to do with affairs of state, and his first visitor was his Secretary of the Congregation of Extraordinary Ecclesiastical Affairs, Monsignor Domenico Tardini. The Home Office was then in charge of Monsignor Giovanni Battista Montini, later Archbishop of Milan.

Pius spent most of the morning conferring with envoys, nuncios, bishops and diplomats from all parts of the world, who came to lay their plans or problems before him, or to present special requests. When the last of the business conferences was over, he received various people, both laymen and clerics of all religions, who had been granted private audiences.

Though Pius was properly jealous of his time and tried to keep his appointments punctually to time, he never gave the slightest impression of pressure. In approaching the Pope a visitor passed through wonderfully decorated halls, shuttled from Swiss Guards to gentlemen-in-waiting, from noble princes to papal chamberlains, but this flurry of traditional pomp was left at the door of his office. For Pius kept the atmosphere there completely informal—he made everyone feel at home.

The Pope sat behind his big desk dressed in a long white cassock and a white skull-cap. He always rose to greet his guests with a smile in his eyes and a welcoming outstretched hand. His thin white fingers looked too delicate to bear the weight of the Fisherman's Ring. His guest might kiss it or simply bend over it, for Pius never stood on formality; he wanted to get as close to people as he could. He seated his guest beside him or across the desk and started the conversation in the visitor's native language on some topic in which he would be interested, for like all good executives Pius was well briefed beforehand. Even the most nervous soon found himself talking as friend to friend as the genuine interest that Pius felt in each visitor warmed his spirit. And each felt as though his audience were the only one that day.

Indeed, the world was—and is—Pius's family, whom he loves regardless of religious difference. One day he received four Protestant ministers from the United States. The conversation was very lively, since Pius was tremendously interested in news from that country. He asked after people he had met in America, and talked of places he had visited and of his hopes for the part he believed America would play in the preservation of world order. In this connection he mentioned his correspondence with the President of the United States. When one of the ministers asked him quizzically, "Are you sure you're not trying to convert him?" the Pope laughed in delight.

These private audiences were far from routine. In the goodness of their hearts people brought the Holy Father some strange gifts. One morning he was made an honorary member of the Newark, N.J., Fire Department and received the badge of office, with proper solemnity and a twinkle in his eyes. That same day somebody gave him a motor scooter.

Like the great gentleman he is, Pius always tries to save people from embarrassment if they make a *faux pas*. One American congressman asked him to bless a packet of medals he had brought, and reaching into his pocket produced a packet of cigarettes. The Pope gravely blessed it. The congressman only noticed his mistake when he started to put it back in his pocket. He turned purple, but the Pope laughed and blessed the medals as well.

On another occasion, a diplomat mentioned having seen a mountain piper waiting in one of the corridors hoping to play for the Pope. Knowing the ambassador's fondness for folk music, the Pope said, "Good, let's go out and hear him now."

They moved to one of the outer rooms, and the diplomatic conversation was continued to the warbling and droning of the pipes.

On a typical day before his illness when the time for the private audiences was over, Pius would prepare to present himself to the crowds waiting for him in the Hall of Benediction if a public audience was scheduled. He always entered the great hall in the *sedia gestatoria*, but almost immediately would leave it to walk among the people. The children present would run to him, and clutch his white cassock, as they had the scarlet one of Cardinal Pacelli in the Borghese Gardens. But when the adults too, like the children, pressed forward, the Swiss Guards had quite a problem to prevent them from trampling on the object of their veneration.

A strange and rather dreadful incident is reported to have occurred at one of these general audiences. As the Holy Father gave his hand to one visitor, the man slid the Fisherman's Ring from his finger. It was so neatly done that Pius never noticed it, until an aghast chamberlain whispered, "Your ring, Holiness!"

Never changing expression the Pope turned back. Standing in front of the thief he said quietly "I think my ring slipped from my finger."

The man opened his trembling hands, showing the great jewel gleaming in his palm. With no more words, Pius gently took the ring and walked away.

The Pope believed in letting it be known that he was interested in all sorts of people. When Fausto Coppi, the professional bicycle champion of Italy, who was the idol of Italian schoolboys, came for an audience, Pius allowed a picture to be taken of him blessing the bicycle. Another picture showed him standing in the midst of a laughing team of professional football players.

Indeed, Pius was—and is—perhaps, the least stuffy of Popes. Everyone could talk to him freely and without constraint. The friendly human being, who was concealed behind the aloof, ascetic figure of the formal processionals, became evident when he mingled with his people, for he seemed to become one of them without losing the dignity and awesomeness of the Vicar of Christ.

He received people of all races and religions and professions—bus drivers, jockeys, tram conductors, actors and actresses, mechanics and millionaires—the world and his wife pass through the portals of the Holy Father's house.

When the general audiences were over, the Holy Father left the clamour and bustle of the Hall of Benediction for the serenity of his own small apartment. Here he ate lunch alone as tradition imposes that a Pontiff must. As soon as Pius entered the dining-room, the canaries went crazy, twittering excitement in all keys. He opened the door of the cage of his favourite songsters who were frantically beating their wings against the wire. They welcomed him with wild swoops around the room, finally perching on his shoulder, where they sat while he ate.

The Pope's lunch usually consisted of a thin soup or *pasta*, followed by a main course mostly made up of vegetables and some fruit. He drank water, flavoured with a little wine.

After lunch he read the papers or a magazine while he sipped a cup of thick, black coffee—*espresso*. If the canaries got bored by his concentration, they might do some violent aerobatics, or trill brilliantly to attract his attention. When he spoke to them they flew straight back to his shoulder.

When his meal was over, Pius retired to his bedroom to nap for an hour, for he knew he needed this refreshment to be able to work hard and late. At about three-thirty he went down to the courtyard of St. Damaso, where an automobile was waiting to take him to the outer gardens. There he left the car and walked along the broad, shady paths, stopping awhile on the top of the Vatican hill, to look over the roofs of Rome and the flat, lush fields of the Campagna. Sometimes he read as he walked along the paths, and sometimes shut the book to enjoy the tranquil feeling that God is very near in a garden.

At five o'clock he returned to his rooms, and said the

Office, the long daily prayer that all priests, even the Pope, must say.

More work followed, until promptly at seven the two Secretaries of the State Department were again announced. They usually stayed with him talking business for an hour. At eight o'clock he dined, sparely as usual—eggs, perhaps, and some vegetables. When he rose from the table he went to his chapel to pray, and then to his desk for more work.

Only a very few intimates ever saw the Pope during these evening hours. His personal confessor, the Reverend Father Bea, a Jesuit, came often. Pius's nephew, Carlo Pacelli, was always welcome; so was Cardinal Spellman, when he came to Rome. Count Galeazzi, Director of Public Works for Vatican City often came as did the Count's half-brother, Professor Ricardo Galeazzi-Lisi, Pius's physician.

There is a characteristic anecdote of the beginning of the friendship between Pacelli and the Galeazzis. When he was still Secretary of State, Cardinal Pacelli was walking down the Via Sistina when he saw a huge painted eye staring down at him from an office building. It was an advertisement hung out by the well-known ophthalmologist, Professor Galeazzi—it is quite ethical for doctors to advertise themselves in Italy. The sign reminded Pacelli that his glasses needed changing. He marched up the stairs to Galeazzi's office.

Much later, on the night he was elected Pope, Pius found that his fall on the stairs had hurt him more than he thought. Mother Pasqualina told him that he ought to see a doctor. "I know only one doctor in Rome," Pius said. "Send for Galeazzi."

That is how an ophthalmologist happened to become the Pope's private physician.

Unless one of his close friends disturbed them, Pius used these quiet evening hours to prepare his speeches, sermons and addresses. He never read his speeches to an audience, for he had an amazing visual memory and could learn a long script in one or two readings. As he described it, "I can see every page of my address. It is photographed on my mind, and all I have to do is read it."

Because Pius liked the personal touch he never allowed anybody to write these speeches for him, typing them out himself on his white machine. Often it was long after midnight before the clacking of his typewriter ceased.

Indeed, in his time of vigour, the Pope often worked eighteen hours a day. The Vatican librarians were amazed at the number of books he read in a week—French, Italian, English, and the classical languages, Latin and Greek.

His late hours were known to the people of the city. People homeward bound from gay parties, the troubled ones who could not sleep, devout pilgrims and harlots, all manner of men and women would stop in Saint Peter's Square to refresh their spirits by looking at the single lighted window in the blank cliff of the Vatican, burning like a beacon over Rome.

*

CHAPTER TWENTY

THE TRUCE OF GOD

IN JUNE, 1948, Pope Pius declared that 1950 would be a Holy Year. This was in accordance with the comparatively recent tradition that a Holy Year be celebrated every twenty-five years so that each generation of the faithful might enjoy the opportunity to purge their sins and benefit by the upward surge of spirit that accompanies the dedication of an entire year to the glory of God. But the institution of a Holy Year itself is a very ancient tradition indeed.

In fact, like so much of Christian usage, it goes back to the Old Testament and the Mosaic Law, which enjoined the Jews to observe every fiftieth year with special rites and worthy acts. The land was not to be ploughed; slaves were free, debts forgiven.

For centuries after Christianity was officially acknowledged by the Roman Empire under Constantine, there was no formal declaration of a Holy or Jubilee Year. However, it was the custom at the end of each century for the faithful to make a pilgrimage to Rome to pay homage to God and to His Vicar on Earth.

In the year 1300 A.D., Boniface VIII became the first Pope officially to proclaim a Year of Jubilee. In his bull he

enumerated the conditions for obtaining the heavenly benefits thereof. To those who made pilgrimage to the Basilicas
of St. Peter and St. Paul and who confessed with a sincere
desire to make amends for their wrong-doing, he promised
a plenary indulgence. This is not a pardon for sins committed, but a remission of the punishment which remains
after the sins have been forgiven.

By Boniface's direction, the Holy Year opened at the Feast
of the Nativity and continued until the following Christmas.
In that era of unquestioning faith it was a cause of great
rejoicing to all Christendom. Dante refers to the Year of
Jubilee in the Divine Comedy, and Giotto painted a fresco
in the Church of St. John Lateran in which Boniface is seen
reading the Bull of Proclamation. The Italian historian
Villani records that there were a hundred thousand pilgrims
in Rome throughout the year, not counting those who stayed
only for a day.

Because of its great spiritual benefits, Pope Clement VI
proclaimed a Holy Year in 1350, cutting the interval to fifty
years. That time so many pilgrims came to Rome that people
slept in the open around great fires built to keep them warm,
and it is said that the innkeepers were so busy feeding the
crowds that they forgot to take money for their services—
though this stretches the imagination rather far. At any rate,
it is officially recorded that there were a million pilgrims in
the city for the feasts of the Ascension and Pentecost alone.

Each Holy Year brought more pilgrims to Rome. In the
seventeenth century Samuel Pepys received a letter from a
friend in Rome who complained that he was unable to get
through the Holy Door on Christmas Eve because the crush
of people was so great; but he consoled himself with having

got away with a piece of stone to support his devotion.

It was Pope Alexander II who planned the ritual for the opening and closing of the Holy Door, which is still used; and Paul II ordained that the Jubilee Year should be held every quarter of a century. The places of pilgrimage were also increased throughout the centuries so that now, in addition to the two great basilicas, pilgrims must also visit the churches of St. John Lateran and St. Mary Major.

Pius was happy that the traditional time for a Holy Year should come at this particular period, for, in addition to the purely spiritual benefits for the faithful, he saw in it an opportunity to forward his hopes for all mankind. He spent many midnight hours at his desk in December, 1949, writing and rewriting his Christmas message to the cardinals, which included the formal announcement of the opening of the Holy Year. Indeed, he worked on it right up to the moment when he had to robe himself and descend to address the convocation of cardinals.

When Pius was dressed, he went back to his desk to add a last minute thought. Then he pressed the buzzer that summoned Monsignori Montini and Tardini, and with them went to address the convocation.

As the Pope stood on the podium facing the scarlet-robed assembly, he was speaking not only to them, but to the world through the battery of microphones that faced him. He began very slowly, with unusual emphasis. This was "God's year," he said, and spoke of the part religion and faith were to play in its celebration. He announced an innovation of his own, saying that the grace of God knew no boundaries nor chains, and decreed that the benfits of the Jubilee could be granted to those who were forced to remain at home for valid reasons, "to those who cannot see, to the sick, the poor, to those in prison and to the faithful of both sexes in those countries in which on account of particular circumstances they are not allowed to undertake the pilgrimage to Rome."

Thus he showed that no Iron Curtain could shut out God.

The whole Catholic world, Pius said, was to besiege the citadel of heaven with continuous prayers during the twelve months; and the purpose of those prayers was to be:

1. The sanctification of souls through prayer and penance and by devotion to Christ and the Church.
2. World peace and the protection of the Holy Places.
3. The defence of the Church against the attacks of her enemies, and for the return of the godless and the unbelievers to Christ.
4. Social justice and charity for the lowly and those in want.

Now Pius began to speak more rapidly. With intense emotion he invited the whole world, of whatever faith, to participate in these objectives and urged, "the return of all peoples to the design planned by God. According to this design, all peoples—in peace and not in war, in joining together and not in isolation, in justice and not in selfishness of extreme nationalism—are intended to form one great human family whose interests are the advancement of the common good, through helping each other, and a just distribution of the goods of this world which were given by God in trust to men. . . .

"In Rome this year will meet groups of pilgrims, which we will not be able to number, of all races from all nations, speaking every language, and of all characters and national customs. Among them there will be those who dealt out death and those who suffered terribly from war; there will be invaders and invaded, the guard of the prison camp and his prisoner. They will all come here under the Truce of God."

Then Pius spoke of his high hopes that this would lead to a better understanding among all peoples and mutual appreciation. Finally, flinging out his arms so that he made a white cross against the dark background, he raised exalted eyes to heaven and prayed: "May this year, made holy by the grace of God Almighty and the intercession of the august Mother of God, of the apostles and all the saints, be the herald of a new era; and grant peace in our days, peace to our souls, peace to families, peace to our lands, and peace to the nations."

Then Pius descended from the podium and went to be robed in his gold encrusted vestments and the Triple Crown. In the courtyard he seated himself in the *sedia gestatoria* and was carried to the portico of St. Peter's.

The long winter dusk was falling and the cold mountain wind was sweeping the crowd in the great piazza when Pius appeared. Forgetting their freezing bodies they shouted their welcome, and he blessed them from the Chair. Then he was set down before the Door, which is to the right of the high bronze gates that open on the nave of St. Peter's. It had been walled up for a quarter of a century.

Stepping from his Chair, the Pontiff took a small golden hammer with an ivory handle and struck the masonry, intoning in Latin, "Open the doors of justice for me!" He struck again and this time sang, "I shall enter Thy House, O Lord!" A third time he struck, and sang, "Open the door for God is with us!"

At the third stroke, masons broke down the wall, and the entrance was revealed through a cloud of plaster dust. The Order of Penitents moved forward on their knees to clear the threshold of débris, while the Holy Father, in his jewelled vestments, prayed aloud, "O God, who through Thy servant Moses did institute the Year of Jubilee and Remission for the people of Israel, mercifully grant us Thy servants that we may joyfully begin this Jubilee Year, instituted by Thy authority through which Thou hast willed to open this Door with solemnity to Thy people, who enter through it to offer their prayers to Thy Majesty, so that having obtained pardon and indulgence of full remission of all our sins, we may attain heavenly glory through the gift of Thy mercy on the day we are called."

Pius stood silent for a moment, then knelt on the threshold and began to chant the 'Te Deum' in a resonant voice. At the end of the first verse he arose from his knees, and, in exaltation, he crossed the threshold alone.

For a few moments nobody moved. Then there was a slow surge towards the door, a motion that communicated itself in a sort of stirring to the vast crowds in the Square. First the cardinals passed through the Holy Door into the great basilica. They were followed by the bishops and other prelates, and after them poured the faithful in their thousands and tens of thousands.

From his lofty throne, Pius watched the pilgrims surging through the door, flooding out through the wide spaces of the great basilica until it was filled to the last crevice. When no other person could cram his way into the cathedral, the Pontiff rose and gave them his blessing, the blessing of a priest and a father.

So, according to the ritual instituted by Pope Paul, the Holy Year began.

It was a year of great exertion for Pius; and of high exaltation. From Christmas Eve, the pilgrims passed through the ancient gates of Rome in uncounted numbers. The old Roman roads were crowded again with all manner of people, hundreds of thousands of whom came from lands the Romans had never heard of. They came in planes and trains, in Cadillacs and donkey carts. Some of them walked, thinking it a greater merit. A group of Irishmen from Dublin walked across the length of England, through France and over the Alpine passes, camping by the roadside at night, refusing the lifts offered them by passing motorists. A man named Yo-Jahn bicycled from Indo-China. Young girls walked unafraid down all the roads that led to Rome.

Looking after the millions of pilgrims was an enormously complicated business. Pius had formed a central committee for this purpose with worldwide branches. Its motto was 'Work for the pilgrims'. It handled the technical problems brilliantly and humanely. Nearly 4,000,000 pilgrim cards were distributed throughout the world. In and around Rome hostels were prepared, clubs were opened, and medical service arranged for. Thirty thousand rooms were put at the disposal of the committee by private home owners, but there were not nearly enough, as over three hundred train-loads of pilgrims arrived each day in addition to other forms of transport. So good-sized towns of tents arose in the fields outside the Aurelian Wall.

Pius had personally taken a part in overseeing the arrangements. He said, "My door is open to every traveller," and he saw to it that the poor who arrived on foot received free board and lodging for a time commensurate with the length of their journey. Convents and monasteries opened their doors at the Pope's request.

For those able to pay something, hostels and camps were subsidised by the Holy See to give shelter and food at very low prices. Pius asked those who had wealth to help those who had not. Many of the nobility opened their palaces to the pilgrims, and the members of the diplomatic corps took them into the embassies.

Special arrangements were made to help travellers who lost their money. Those who had spent their all to get to Rome and then became ill found that their hospital bills were paid by order of the Holy Father, and in extreme cases they were flown back to their homes.

Rome became a city of prayer. Through the open doors of the great basilicas and the little old forgotten churches came the vibrations of those silent prayers. People prayed in groups, and they prayed alone. They prayed in almost every language used by man; but the prayers were the same.

The diversity of the crowd pleased Pius so much that he did not mind the tremendous physical strain at all. As he looked down on the Square from his windows, he saw African chieftains in nodding feathers, Gauchos who seemed to have stepped straight off Argentine cow ponies, saffron-kilted Irishmen, sports-shirted Americans, Polynesians, Chinese and very nearly every other segment of the human race represented in the long queues that, extending as far as he could see, moved slowly towards the Holy Door. There before his eyes was proof that the Church was, indeed, universal and supra-national.

Of course, all these pilgrims wanted to see their Pope, and Pius made extreme exertions to accommodate them. He held large public audiences three or four times a week, and innumerable private and semi-private audiences every day. At one of the former, as he entered the Hall of Audience, he was delighted to hear a little boy shout excitedly, "Here is my Pope!"

It is estimated that Pius received in audience nearly 3,000,000 people between one Christmas and the next. It was the happiest year of his life.

Though the important part of Pius's life was on an immensely spiritual plane, it was complemented by his vigorous intelligence. In the midst of religious exaltation, he did not abandon intellectual activity. With so many brilliant men of all fields coming to Rome, Pius considered that a great opportunity would be lost if they did not get together for discussions of mundane, but none the less important, matters. At his suggestion literary men met to read their works. Music, which was his first love among the arts, was represented by a conference of leading musicians from many countries. There were also meetings of journalists, sociologists, artists, and, indeed, there were discussions of most of the things with which the minds and emotions of men are concerned. Because of his interest in modern innovations, Pius also encouraged a Motion Picture Congress.

The administrative affairs of a great world-wide Church also pressed upon Pius. Several thousand bishops came to Rome, each heading a flock of penitential pilgrims. The bishops left their croziers, symbols of authority, behind and carried simple wooden crosses. But they could not leave the cares of their dioceses so easily. Pius tried to see all of them, and to advise each on his particular problems. These talks ranged from discussions of politics and finance, to such questions as modernising seminaries, vocations, youth, and social action.

In addition to all these extra duties and conferences, there remained the great annual ceremonials of the Church which the Supreme Pontiff must perform. Of these the celebration of the Pentecost was that year one of the most moving. For this occasion Pius was dressed in red vestments, with his cardinals and bishops in the same triumphant hue. The polished marble of St. Peter's seemed to glow with reflected colour, and the eyes of the crowd shone with the flame of spiritual unity.

This was the occasion Pius had chosen for one of the most moving rites of the Church, a canonisation that had been in preparation for many years by the Congregation of Rites. Speaking so clearly that everyone could hear his words, Pius porclaimed that, "In honour of the Holy and Undivided Trinity, for the exaltation of the Church and the growth of the Christian religion, with the authority of our Lord Jesus Christ, of the blessed apostles Peter and Paul, and Our own; after mature deliberation and having frequently implored Divine Aid, upon counsel of our venerable brethren, the Cardinals of the Holy Roman Church, the Patriarchs, Archbishops and Bishops present in the City, We decree and define Maria Goretti a saint, and inscribe her in the list of saints, laying down that her memory be recalled with pious devotion every year. In the name of the Father and of the Son and of the Holy Ghost."

Pius had in mind an even more important pronouncement to make in this Holy Year. This was the proclamation of a new dogma. There is an extraordinary misconception among Catholics as well as Protestants and those of other religions as to the infallibility of the Pope. According to the tenets of the Catholic Church, the Pope can be as wrong as anyone else in most matters, and it is no sin to disagree with him. It is only when he solemnly speaks *ex-cathedra* on faith or morals, that the Supreme Pontiff is held to be infallible.

The proclamation of a new dogma is an act that is seldom done. Not since the days of Pius IX, nearly a hundred years before, had a Pope thus defined a new article of faith. On November 1, 1950, Pius proclaimed the Dogma of the Assumption of the Virgin. This is the dogma that the body of the Mother of God was not permitted to disintegrate like those of ordinary mortals, but was raised directly to heaven as was that of her Son.

The gentle Virgin had been the object of special veneration to Pius all his life. But like all Popes he did not act entirely on his own initiative. Belief in the Assumption had persisted since earliest times, both in the Eastern and Western Churches. Before his proclamation of the new dogma, Pius had instructed his clerical scholars to examine all the evidence minutely, and to interpret it for him. Not only that, but he found that the belief is an inescapable logical conclusion from the doctrine of the Immaculate Conception. In proclaiming the Dogma of the Assumption, Pius acted on logical grounds, and was officially confirming a belief long held. The Pope's own personal feeling was a mystical conviction of the divine truth of this dogma.

Indeed, speaking officially before a great crowd in Lisbon,

the Pope's closest friend, Frederick Cardinal Tedeschini, told of how, on October 31, 1950, the eve of his proclamation of the Dogma of the Assumption, the Holy Father was walking in the Vatican gardens at about four o'clock in the afternoon, when looking upward he saw "the sun dancing in the sky".

On Christmas Eve, 1950, Pius was again reviewing his annual message to the cardinals, and re-living the triumphant happenings of the Holy Year. But though it had seen an even greater resurgence of faith than he had dared to hope for, there was a dark side to the picture. War had broken out again in Korea. And Pius was painfully conscious of those who had been prevented from making the holy pilgrimage by the regulations of Communist countries, of hundreds of bishops and hundreds of thousands of the faithful locked behind that grim Curtain. So when he spoke to the cardinals he cried in an impassioned voice, "Away with barriers! Down with barbed-wire fences! Let all people be free to know the lives of others! Let segregation of some countries . . . so dangerous to the cause of peace, be destroyed! For the Church, East and West do not represent different ideals but a common heritage . . . The divine mission of the Church makes her a mother to all peoples, and a trustworthy ally and a wise guide to all who look for peace. . . .

"If there is any place left where peace can be found, it is here in this place, sanctified by the blood of the apostles and martyrs, and where the Vicar of Christ acknowledges no duty more sacred, no mission more satisfying, than that of being the untiring herald of peace."

When he had finished speaking, Pius was again robed in

his vestments of ceremony; and was carried on the high, swaying Chair, to the Holy Door. Here he descended and walked alone through the sacred entrance. Then mounting the *sedia gestatoria* again, he was carried through the crowded basilica to the Chapel of the Blessed Sacrament. As he prayed there in silence, the whole vast congregation soundlessly left the cathedral through the Holy Door. The prelates, bishops and cardinals followed them.

When the great church was empty, Pius arose from his knees, and passed through the Holy Door for the last time. On the portico, he faced towards the Door, while a Penitent put a stonemason's apron over his vestments. Then taking a trowel in his long slender hand, Pius made three little piles of mortar on the threshold—to the right, to the left and in the centre. Then he took a golden brick from another of the Order of Penitents, and placed it in the centre of the Door; then one to the right and to the left. On their knees the Penitents laid more bricks in the opening.

After that a canvas screen was placed across the archway to symbolise its closing. As this was done Pius on his knees prayed aloud, "O God, Who lendest a benign and merciful ear throughout Thy Kingdom, hear us we beseech Thee, and make it so that the sanctity of this spot remains inviolate, and that all the faithful may rejoice at having obtained the blessings of Thy gifts in this Year of Jubilee."

He remained for a long moment, a small white figure kneeling under the high arches of the portico. Then rising he intoned the 'Te Deum' in ringing tones. After the triumphant hymn, he raised his hand, giving his blessing to the four quarters of the world. And he left St. Peter's.

*

CHAPTER TWENTY-ONE

THE VISION

THE period immediately following the Holy Year was in a sense a time of recession for Pius. To the Korean War was added fighting in Indo-China. Everywhere the Communists seemed to be advancing. Sometimes the Pope must have felt that he was fighting a rearguard action against the forces of darkness—though he fought no less vigorously because of that.

In addition, he became ever more aware of his failing physique. He was ageing suddenly as men sometimes do who have remained vigorous beyond their normal expectation. Not that Pius would permit so small a thing as the infirmities of the body to slow him down. He worked as hard as ever, and his mind functioned with all its customary cogency. The net effect of his body's weakness seemed to be that his spirit became stronger so that more and more it transcended his never robust flesh.

Meanwhile, he worked primarily for peace. In April, 1951, he received delegates of the Universal Movement for World Confederation. He told them that he approved in general of their organisation, but warned them against a mechanical and forced unification that took into account merely numbers and quantities, forgetting the personal aspirations of man. There must, he said, be an 'order of liberty'.

Conversely, when he talked to members of the *Pax Christi,* the Catholic peace movement, he told them that the Church alone could not bring about peace, but could do so only by co-operation with political forces. "The Church cannot stand aloof, or remain indifferent, nor have recourse only to prayer. It must co-operate in the work for peace."

Realistically, Pius recognised that the youth of the free world had become weary and sceptical, whereas Communist youth seemed enthusiastic for the false doctrines they were taught. This, he felt, called for much more strenuous efforts on the part of the Church and the leaders of the democracies. Taking a step in this direction he secured an agreement with the Italian Government permitting the Holy See to build two new extra-territorial radio transmitters at Castel Romano and Santa Maria di Galeria about twelve miles north and south of Rome.

Pius also continued to work for the integration of Europe, which he had supported in 1948. When the Consultative Assembly of the Council of Europe met in Strasbourg in 1952, the Pope sent the Dean of the Sacred College, Cardinal Tisserant, there to represent him. Pius made it clear that he favoured any sort of integration, economic and political, but he insisted that spiritual values must have recognition.

Further to emphasise the universality of the Church, Pius created a number of new cardinals in 1953, bringing the Sacred College up to its full complement of seventy members. Twenty-seven nations were now represented in it. Thirteen cardinals were from the Americas, and the

Italians, who formerly had a large majority, held only twenty-six seats.

The consistory took place on January 15, 1953. At it Pius defied the Communists and recognised the services of two modern martyrs by making Archbishops Stepinac of Yugoslavia and Wyszynski of Poland Princes of the Church—he had already raised Mindszenty of Hungary. Neither Poland nor Yugoslavia would allow the Archbishops to go to Rome, so their Red Hats were sent to them.

The Communists were, of course, enraged. Yugoslavia broke off diplomatic relations with the Holy See, and in Poland Wyszynski was arrested and thrown into prison.

Though his strength was visibly failing throughout this year, Pius continued to be extremely active, nor did the variety of his interests diminish. In October, he gave an audience to the delegates attending a convention of the American Society of Travel Agents which was held in Rome. The Pope spoke to these men in English of his nostalgia for his own days of travel, and particularly of his visit to America. With a glint of quiet humour, he commented that "Though our direct contacts with your esteemed confraternity during recent years have been understandably few, we still treasure the memory of many an early courteous service rendered."

Then he went on to tell them that their opportunities for dedication to the service of people were many and their responsibilities before divine law serious. "Travel of one sort or another has assumed the proportions of a quest for personal fulfilment," he said, "and your duty is to help this fulfilment." Then he added a quotation from Tennyson's 'Ulysses' that aptly tallied with his own experiences of travel

—"For always roaming with a hungry heart, much have I seen and known."

The Roman autumn was soft and golden that year, but Pius's strength was sinking. He had worked hard all his life, and the fifteen years of his pontificate had been a time of unremitting struggle and worry. Throughout, he had been torn by anxiety for the safety of the world; and by anguish for those of his children whom he could not save. All his close associates expressed wonder that so frail and ascetic a man could survive the load of work and worry he imposed upon himself.

Pius did not consider it remarkable at all. He expressed his real opinion of himself when he said to Bishop Fulton J. Sheen, "As a man, I am nothing."

The year 1954 brought both the ebb tide of the Holy Father's strength, and his almost miraculous recovery. He had designated it a Marian Year, that is a year dedicated to the Virgin Mother, in honour of the centenary of the definition of the Dogma of the Immaculate Conception. And he urged the faithful particularly to pray for peace to Her who was the Mother of Peace.

Early in the year Pius suffered a severe attack of hiccups which, together with other internal disorders, weakened him painfully. From that time on he was a very sick man, though his ardent spirit kept him working at what would have been a tremendous pace for a youth in the first strength of manhood. No matter was too trivial or too great for his attention.

In January, when the new Minister from Great Britain to the Holy See presented his credentials, Pius made a graceful speech recalling the time he had received the then Princess

Elizabeth in audience. Now that God had placed the weight of empire on her youthful shoulders, the Pope said he was sure that the young queen's courageous simplicity would conquer all obstacles.

However, Pius was so ill that his attendants had to half carry him from the audience. His weight had dropped rapidly for he could eat very little and he was suffering extreme pain.

On February 14, from his bed, Pius began to deliver a radio talk to comfort those who, like himself, were very ill and confined to their rooms. In it he particularly spoke to young people who, in their sense of the injustice of their ills asked, "Why should a good God condemn me to suffer?"

He pointed out to them that God had permitted his Son to suffer on the Cross, yet what evil had He done? Pointing a fragile finger at the picture of the Madonna, he spoke of Mary's spiritual anguish and said, "She did not curse. She did not ask God why. She and her Son suffered voluntarily in full conformity with the divine design. You may be suffering for others or for yourselves, so learn to utter the 'so be it' of resignation and patience."

The Pope was so weak that in the middle of a sentence his voice failed, and one of the attending priests had to continue reading the script.

Nevertheless, by early March Pius had written ten major addresses. The first of these dealt with the subject of television. He considered it a great gift of science, but saw its dangers clearly. It could bring the whole family together, or it could bring disruption and discord into the home. "Television is directed to family groups so that at any hour in any place it is capable of moving the emotions, particularly those of youth," he pointed out. "It finds its most rapt devotees among children and adolescents. The family as the cell of society must be preserved, and public authorities have the duty of taking every precaution that the home be in no way offended or disturbed. Did not even pagan Juvenal say that 'for the child one must have the utmost reverence'?"

By May, Pius was a little better—very little. But he was utterly determined to perform a ceremony in which love and duty were combined, and which he considered one of the most important acts of his Pontificate. This was the canonisation of Pope Pius X.

As always in such cases, the life of the peasant Pope had been subjected to the most rigorous examination, his two miracles of healing had been attested and the conclusion had been affirmed that he was, indeed, worthy of a place among the elect. Pius had performed the beatification ceremony in 1951. Now was the time for the final moving rite that would make the simple, humble man, who always considered himself 'unworthy', St. Pius X.

Dr. Galeazzi was horrified. It was incredible that his patient could muster strength for the long exhausting part he must play. Pius was resolute. This was a thing he felt he must do, and if it were the last act of his life, well, it was still worth doing. God would give him strength.

So the canonisation was fixed for May 29, 1954.

As always, the Pope stood patiently during the hour-long robing in his heavy vestments. That he could do so in his frail condition was itself a minor miracle, and indeed at times he seemed to sway from fatigue. Then he went to the Sistine Chapel, where, surrounded by the College of

Cardinals, he spent some time in prayer. There he was twice asked to make Pius X a saint. According to ritual, he made no reply, but intoned the *Ave Maris Stella*.

Now Pius mounted the *sedia gestatoria*, and was carried in procession through the massed crowds in St. Peter's Square. Ahead marched hundreds of prelates in ascending order of rank from simple monks and priests to cardinals. Then came the Swiss Guards, their cuirasses flashing in the strong spring sunshine, and after them the Noble Guard in golden helmets.

As the Pope reached the high doors of St. Peter's, Cardinal Cicognani for the third time asked him to make Pius X a saint, and this time the Pope indicated his assent. Then he was enthroned on the terrace before the central door of St. Peter's.

Pius has never told of the stress he endured during that long ceremony, or of the faintness that at times threatened to overcome him. But his doctor, who was close at hand, was obliged to give him restoratives at times. Despite his weakness the Pope's voice was clear and resonant as he sang *Oremus* and read the decree of canonisation, as it was later when he pronounced the superb panegyric he had written about St. Pius X.

The following day, there was the equally impressive—and exhausting—ceremony of the Mass of Canonisation. St. Peter's was crowded to its utmost capacity, and again the Pope took his full part in the ritual. His people never guessed how spent he was, for the frail figure in the glittering vestments seemed as firm as ever; the head that wore the heavy Triple Crown remained erect.

At last the silver trumpets blared the signal for his departure, and the great chair under its golden canopy was carried to the door. There the bearers turned, and Pius, facing the immense crowded nave, once more gave his blessing to his people. Of that moment Father Francis Thornton has written, "Never had he seemed more magnetic. All hearts were drawn to him." It was the ultimate triumph of spirit over failing flesh.

Soon after the canonisation the Pope went to Castel Gandolfo. He hoped that perhaps the good air of his beloved countryside would work its customary cure, and that he would regain strength enough to continue the fight against the forces that threatened to embroil the Church and the world. The serenity of the ancient palace was in keeping with his own tranquil resignation. But the symptoms of his illness continued with their torturing pain. Though he had to cut down on his audiences, he stayed at work. When his doctors begged him to take life easier, he smiled gently and said, "A Pope must work until he dies."

The summer of 1954 was long and hot. But in the course of it Pius wrote twelve more major speeches on various subjects, all of which required much research. This made a total of twenty-two long, thoughtful addresses written by the Pope in the first nine months of his illness.

It was not until November 27 that Pius came back to the Vatican. He was literally a wraith. Nearly a year had passed since he had been taken ill. From a normal one hundred and forty-five pounds his weight was down to one hundred and five pounds. The violent hiccuping had returned and he could neither eat nor retain food. As he lay breathing shallowly on his narrow bed, his skin was so white and drawn it appeared translucent. Only his black eyes were still lighted by intelligence and his indomitable spirit. Indeed in those final days of November, he seemed to have shed his last physical attributes and to be *all* spirit.

The Pope's physicians were in despair. Dr. Galeazzi-Lisi, who had taken care of him for so long, had before this called in other physicians, the principal ones being Dr. Paolucci and Dr. Gasbarrini. In all some eighteen doctors were in consultation. They spoke of peritonitis; or failing kidneys. They talked of an operation that they knew was impossible. In the end all they could decide was that there was nothing they could do.

On the evening of December 1, 1954, virtually all hope was given up. Pius was too weak to lift his hand. What life remained in his body was the faintest flicker of animation; his heart-beat was no stronger than a dying butterfly's wing-stroke; his breathing barely sufficient to cloud a mirror. All the world knew he was dying. In the churches of Christendom, not only those of the Catholic faith, but Orthodox Greek and Protestant as well, people were praying for the man whom they, whatever their religion, felt to be the most Christ-like of our time. On that bleak winter evening in the great Square of St. Peter's people of all nations, who happened to be in Rome, were kneeling on the pavement under the windswept corner of the Vatican where they knew the Holy Father lay. They bowed their heads in prayer; and raised them to look up at the narrow windows on the third floor where they had so often seen his light burning over Rome. They looked for a sign.

In the Square, too, were camera crews from all the big news agencies setting up their equipment to record the dramatic moment of the Pope's death. The bustle they made struck an incongruous note in the mournful silence. It seemed somehow ghoulish. Yet had Pius known they were there he would not have minded. For he would have realised that they were doing their jobs; and he was ever one to believe that it was vitally important that truthful facts should be disseminated as quickly as possible. And he would have realised that his own death would be important news.

Pius also felt that he was dying. Despite his weakness, his mind was crystal clear, and he was not the person to fool himself with illusory hopes. Indeed, it is doubtful if hope is the word; for he was very tired. If hope there was, it is more probable that he hoped that now he would be permitted to lay down the burden.

Pius's expectation of death was strengthened later that evening. He was quite alone for a moment when he heard a Voice say, "There will be a vision!"

One can only dimly imagine the exaltation that those words brought to him. They were the proof that he had indeed found favour in the eyes of his Lord. In the wonderful assurance of that knowledge, he gave thanks, and contentedly, like a tired child, he fell asleep.

Pius woke very early on the morning of December 2. In the light reflected from the street lamps in the Square and the strengthening dawn he could see quite clearly all the familiar details of his room. He knew that he was weaker than ever and, believing that his time was nearly spent, he began to recite a favourite prayer, *'Anima Christi'*—'Soul of Christ'.

As he reached the words *"in hora mortis meae voca me"**

* In the hour of my death call Thou me.

he saw the Saviour standing by his bedside, "silent in all His eloquent majesty."

Pius thought that, as long ago He had come for Peter saying "Follow me," Jesus had come for him. Joyfully the Holy Father spoke to him. *"O bone Jesu!"* he said with all his heart and soul, *"O bone Jesu! Voca me; iube me venire ad Te!"**

Albeit, gentle Jesus had not come to summon Pius, but to comfort him. And after a little while He went away.

* O good Jesus! O good Jesus! Call Thou me; order me to come to Thee!

A PROTESTANT LOOKS AT
THE POPE

A LAST WORD
by
ALDEN HATCH

THIS is not an age of miracles. Indeed it is so sceptical that a miracle seems downright anachronistic. When the Vision of Eugenio Pacelli was made public nearly a year later, on November 18, 1955, there was a howl of unbelief. This was due in part to the manner of its presentation.

The first account of it was written by Luigi Cavicchioli for the Italian picture magazine *Oggi*. It caused a world-furore. Vatican telephones rang all day. The small staff was swamped by calls from the news media of the whole world. All of them got the same answer—"no comment."

Since the Vatican never deigns to reply to any statement made about the Pope, this was the equivalent of a denial. For two days poor Cavicchioli was the most discredited reporter in the word.

Pius had not intended that the news should be made public in his lifetime. With his usual common sense he envisioned the controversy it would arouse. However, the Pope had confided the story of his vision to a few intimate friends—what human being could help it? One of these must have talked to Cavicchioli; for the *Oggi* story was substantially correct. Pius could not conscientiously allow a newspaperman, however indiscreet, to suffer for telling the truth. On November 21, 1955, he ordered the Vatican press director, Luciano Casmiri, to confirm the truth of Cavicchioli's story.

Just as Pius had foreseen, the announcement produced a storm of sceptical comment. Though he was braced for it, the Holy Father was deeply hurt by this reaction. Fortunately it was not universal. Far more people accepted it as simple truth. At his next public audience the crowd emotionally cried *"Viva il sante Papa!"*

In its issue of December 4, 1955, *L'Osservatore della Domenica,* the Sunday counterpart of the Vatican paper *L'Osservatore Romano,* published the *official* story of the vision. It was probably written or authenticated by Pius himself. This account has been scrupulously followed herein.

Though the present writer is a Protestant, he believes that he has an unbiased point of view. Nevertheless there will be no attempt here to assay evidence. Stark facts will be presented.

Certainly there can be no doubt of Pius's story. He is a man of truth. Certainly, also, a man so ill could have an hallucination. And yet . . .

Two mornings after the vision, when the doctors came to see their 'hopeless' patient, he greeted them with the words, "Good morning, gentlemen, I am happy to see you." Three weeks later Pius was writing his Christmas message to the world, and, though he was not yet strong enough to deliver it on Christmas Day, he gave it over the radio early in January. It was another carefully researched, closely reasoned appeal for peace. One section alone shows that his mind was as vigorous as ever. Speaking of the cold peace he said, "The main basis on which the present state of calm rests is fear. Each nation tolerates the existence of the other because it does not itself wish to perish. The most obvious absurdity of this is that politics, while dreading war, at the same time puts all its trust in war.

"The present co-existence in fear has therefore only two ends before it. It can raise itself to co-existence in fear of God and thus lead to a life of peacefulness inspired by Divinity; or it can dry more and more into a frozen nothingness of international life. . . ."

Certainly Pius had no hallucinations about international affairs.

Certainly the Pope's recovery could be called miraculous. On January 7, he created Monsignor Montini, his pro-secretary of state, an archbishop and sent him to Milan. This was like cutting off his own right hand, for Montini had been his closest associate for over fifteen years and was invaluable to him. It meant adding greatly to the work the Pope himself must do. But Pius thought that Montini would be more valuable combatting Communism among the Milanese workers than at the Vatican, and he felt strong enough to spare him.

Indeed, Pius was soon more vigorous than he had been for years. During 1955, he received over 380,000 people in audience, and delivered sixty major addresses. Among those he received in private audience were American Secretary of State John Foster Dulles, Premier Jawaharlal Nehru of India, Prime Minister John Costello of Ireland, and various royal princes—among them King Mutara Ludahigwa of Ruanda-Urundi. Though Pius was a tall man, the seven-foot African king in his white-plumed headdress set with pearls towered over him. The king, almost in tears, said that it was the most moving day of his life.

Of the Pope's sixty speeches, thirty-one were in Italian, twenty-two in French, six in English and one in Portuguese. The subjects covered ranged from purely religious topics to international affairs and the need for more automobile express-ways. Pius also covered the question of psychiatry, clarifying the Church's attitude towards it. He decreed that the religious orders be permitted to modernise their traditional costumes and personally approved new designs for nuns' habits to enable them to take a more active part in the modern world.

It was indeed a busy year in which Pius served his Master well. But he continued to increase his activities. For example, in May, 1956, he received more than 200,000 people in audience and delivered seventeen major speeches. Indicating that his desire for the alleviation of the troubles of age was as intense as his interest in those of young people, he gave a long audience to Dr. George Sperti of the American Society for the Aged in which he discussed the topic with his usual acumen and revealed his intimate knowledge of special American conditions. The result was to inspire Dr. Sperti to redouble his efforts on behalf of those who faced the lonely failing years of life.

While such a remarkable come-back does not prove a miracle, certainly it indicates something. Of course, the treatments prescribed by the Pope's physicians helped. And in due course they received high Papal decorations for their services. But it is nearly inconceivable that those despairing doctors could have effected the cure unaided by some outside Power.

One of the facts that must also be reckoned with is the character of Pius himself. Here was no mere visionary dreaming dreams upon a windswept hillside; but a man trained in logic and the evaluation of events, with a profound knowledge of philosophy and history, especially the history of religion. He knew very well how fantastically improbable it was that he should see Christ. There is no record of a Pope having seen the Saviour since the first Pope, Peter, nearly two thousand years ago. Only a small number of great mystics have ever claimed to have seen Him in all those centuries. St. Teresa of Avila, St. Gertrude, St. Margaret Mary. . . . These are some of the favoured few of times past who have set down for us their rare visions.

Pius, a very humble man, could have had no expectation—no hope even—that so great a sign of Divine favour would be accorded him. Pius is a man of truth. Pius says he saw the Lord. . . .

Many years must pass before a man or an event can be truly weighed in the scales of history. Contemporary opinions are so influenced by the emotions and prejudices of their particular era as to be at best merely corroborative evidence in the eyes of a future historian. But that historian, writing in some distant unimaginable future, will have plenty of evidence of one thing: It is that throughout the world people of all races and of every religion, in fact very nearly everyone who had any faith in God, were agreed that Eugenio Pacelli was the most saintly man of our time.

INDEX

225, 227, 228, 240 (*see also* Marxism)
Communist Revolution, 75
Congregation of Extraordinary Ecclesiastical Affairs, 41, 207 (*see also* Vatican Foreign Office)
Congregation of Ordinary Ecclesiastical Affairs, 41
Congregation of Rites, 223
Constantine the Great, 93, 99, 107, 203, 214
Consultative Assembly, 228
Conte di Savoia, 113
Conte Grande, 107, 109
Coppi, Fausto, 210
Corso Vittorio Emmanuele, 140, 156, 199
Costello, John, 240
Council of Europe, 228
Court of St. James's, 46, 53
Crusade of Charity, 174, 181
Cuba, 185
Czechoslovakia, 80, 124, 137, 192

Dalla Costa, Cardinal, 8
Dante, Alighieri, 215
De Gaspari, Alcide, 166
Della Chiesa, Giacomo Cardinal, 41, 59
Denmark, 148
De Valera, Eamon, 136
Diamare, Bishop Gregorio, 173
Di Belmonte, Cardinal, 9
Dogma of the Assumption of

the Virgin, 224–5
Dogma of the Immaculate Conception, 224, 230
Dulles, John Foster, 240

East Prussia, 61
Ebert, Friedrich, 79, 82
Eden, Anthony, 154
Edward VII, King of England, 46
Egypt, 153
Eisner, Kurt, 75
Elizabeth, Princess, 231
England, 53, 54, 55, 56, 72, 98, 139, 142, 152, 182, 185
  armed forces, 159
  Eighth Army, 163, 170, 176
Erzberger, Deputy, 72
Ethiopia, 109, 110

Farinacci, Roberto, 163
Fascism, 97, 103, 149
Finland, 144
Fisherman's Ring, the, 2, 37, 58, 65, 208, 210
Florence, 145
Fordham University, 96
Foreign Office (*see* Vatican Foreign Office)
Forum, the, 140
Four Freedoms, the 191
France, 55, 57, 60, 61, 72, 83, 105, 139, 142, 149, 185
Francis-Ferdinand, Archduke, 57
Franco, Francisco, 117

Mass of Canonisation, 233
Mazzini, Giuseppe, 14
Merry del Val, Raphael Cardinal, 50, 53–4, 56, 57, 58, 59, 98
  Secretary of State, 53
Mexico, 105
Michaelis, George, 71–2
Michelangelo, 99, 164
Mikhailovitch, Gen. Draja, 195
Mindszenty, Joseph Cardinal, 196, 229
Monte Cassino, 173
Monte Giordano, 127
Monte Soratte, 87
Montini, Msgr. Giovanni Battista, 137, 156, 157, 207, 216, 242
Morosini, Don Giuseppe, 173
Moscow, 152
Motion Picture Congress, 222
Mount Vernon, 114
Mundelein, George Cardinal, 118
Munich Pact, 137
Mussolini, Benito, 88, 89, 102–3, 104, 110, 118, 122, 123, 138, 142, 146, 147–8, 150, 154, 158, 163
Mutara Ludahigwa, King of Ruanda-Urundi, 240

NAPLES, 163
Napoleon Bonaparte, 42
Napoleon III, 15
National Press Club, 114

Nazism, 68, 83–4, 97, 101, 105, 111, 118
Nehru, Jawaharlal, 240
Nenni, Pietro, 166
Neo-Fascists, 163, 165, 168
Nero, 98
Newark N.J., Fire Department, 209
New York City, 113, 114, 145
Niagara Falls, 115
Nicholas II, Czar of Russia, 43
Noble Guard, 233
Norfolk, Duke of, 136
North American College, 54
Norway, 148
Notre Dame, 114
Notre Dame de Paris, 121

O'FLAHERTY, MSGR. HUGH, 168–70
Oggi, 238–9
Onano, 13, 27, 28, 29, 34, 35, 39, 188
Oreglia, Cardinal, 49
Orsenigo, Archbishop Cesare, 139, 143
Osservatore della Domenica L', 203, 239
Osservatore Romano, L', 15, 148, 149, 163, 203, 239

PACELLI, CARLO, 147, 152, 212
Pacelli, Elizabetta, 21
Pacelli, Eugenio:
  activities, 202–13
  apprendista, 46

248